YOU ARE
LOVED & FREE

YOU ARE
LOVED & FREE

A GUIDED JOURNEY TO WINNING THE BATTLE
FOR YOUR IDENTITY

REDEMPTION
PRESS

MICAH RUTH

Published by Redemption Press, PO Box 427, Enumclaw, WA 98022.

Toll-Free (844) 2REDEEM (273-3336)

Redemption Press is honored to present this title in partnership with the author. The views expressed or implied in this work are those of the author. Redemption Press provides our imprint seal representing design excellence, creative content, and high-quality production.

Unless otherwise indicated, all Scripture quotations are taken from the Holy Bible, New Living Translation, copyright © 1996, 2004, 2015 by Tyndale House Foundation. Used by permission of Tyndale House Publishers, Inc., Carol Stream, Illinois 60188. All rights reserved.

Scripture quotations marked MSG are taken from The Message, copyright © 1993, 2002, 2018 by Eugene H. Peterson. Used by permission of NavPress. All rights reserved. Represented by Tyndale House Publishers, Inc.

Scripture quotations marked NIV are taken from the Holy Bible, New International Version®, NIV® Copyright ©1973, 1978, 1984, 2011 by Biblica, Inc.® Used by permission. All rights reserved worldwide.

ISBN: 978-1-64645-047-3 (Paperback)
978-1-64645-048-0 (ePub)
978-1-64645-049-7 (Mobi)

Library of Congress Catalog Card Number: 2020908019

Dedicated to my brilliant daughter who, like all of us, struggles with feeling loved and being free to be the woman God created her to be. The cry of my heart is that she finds freedom much sooner than the thirty-seven years it took me.

CONTENTS

A GOD-ORDAINED MIDLIFE CRISIS

*Long before he laid down earth's foundations, he had us
in mind, had settled on us as the focus of his love, to be
made whole and holy by his love. Long, long ago he decided to adopt us into his family through Jesus Christ. (What
pleasure he took in planning this!) He wanted us to enter
into the celebration of his lavish gift-giving by the hand
of his beloved Son.*
Ephesians 1:4–5 MSG

THE TRAJECTORY OF MY LIFE took a distinct turn when I finally fell
to my knees in surrender to God. I found the path to freedom
through a midlife crisis, divinely planned by God to show me how
wrongly I was identifying myself. In the pages of Ephesians lay the
secret to rebuilding my identity in Christ as a loved and free daugh-

ter of God. Those pages also provided me with the armor I needed to walk in my created purpose.

You see, before this season I did not understand the ongoing battle for my identity. I didn't even know who I was battling. I was lost in the American way of finding value and worth in the approval of others and in my accomplishments. I worked hard in all areas of my life to prove I was significant and valuable, relentlessly striving to earn our culture's definition of success: a great job, a picture-perfect family, and a flawless appearance. I looked like the can-do-it-all female who had it all together all the time. However, God's message of truth was clouded by my vision of success, which I failed to measure up to despite my efforts. I knew the constant striving was destroying my soul, hurting my family, and killing my dreams. But I did not know another way.

Despite becoming a Christian in my late twenties, over a decade prior, I still worked to prove I was good enough to be loved. I had not rebuilt my identity in Christ, let alone believed it. The Enemy and our culture had convinced me that hard work and worldly success would give me self-worth, because people would then approve of me. But it was never enough. I couldn't overcome my deep sense of worthlessness and restlessness. Struggling year after year only tightened my chains and forced me to work harder and harder to keep up the facade.

By the time God sent me to my knees, I was going to such extremes to seek approval that I was breaking. Pieces of me splintered all over the place. This had become painfully obvious to me and to everyone else, even as I pretended everything was fine.

But God, in His amazing love, wanted better for me.

He wants better for you too.

Just as I expected a promotion for all my hard work at my job, God instead walked me through a hard demotion experience to reveal my skewed beliefs and to set me on a new path. He wanted me to know I was worthy because the Creator of the universe made and redeemed me, not because of anything I accomplished. And certainly not because of a man-made title. The demotion was the only way God could open my eyes to the battle for my identity. Through it, I finally saw how blindly I followed the world's broken ways and how completely I believed the Enemy's lies.

As I processed my demotion at work, God revealed to me the core reason I worked to prove my value: deep down, I had never truly believed I was good enough. Like many others, I was shamed about my weight as a child and suffered hard moments that tattooed identities on my heart: *rejected, betrayed,* and *not good enough.* With the Enemy's assistance, I carried these lies with me into adulthood, my failed first marriage, my career, my parenting, and even my relationship with God.

But He had a plan to use this demotion to bring about healing and redemption.

After a few tough days filled with searching and tears, a new devotional appeared in my email. It was a gift from God: a devotional series on Ephesians. The first devotional in the series was based on Ephesians 1:4–5 and was undeniably written for me and for this exact moment. I read and reread it, shaking with the irrefutable knowledge that God was in the room and that this devo was the answer to my soul's cry.

A few days later, our church started studying Ephesians as well. I knew God had answers for me, and He'd give them to me if I would surrender to Him and study the book of Ephesians.

So I did. I agreed to trust God's plan for this hard season and dig into Ephesians. He took me on a journey to the center of my heart and opened my eyes to new truths that changed everything. As I dug in, I recognized the war on my identity. I learned why the Enemy uses our identities to keep us from God's best. I saw my heart, full of badly bandaged wounds and infected from a lack of healing. These wounds had poisoned every area of my life.

God showed me how these wounds, twisted by the Enemy,

had become both my identity and my armor. Best of all, I saw that God wanted to heal me and rebuild my identity on the truth found in Ephesians: that I am created uniquely and loved dearly by the God who sent His only Son to win me back to Himself (Ephesians 1:4–5). And as each chapter of Ephesians unfolded, I found the processes of deep-soul transformation that restored me to my true self, developed a deeper relationship with my Creator, and put on the armor I needed to walk in freedom and be the real me.

Heart transformation is God's plan, His doing, and His pleasure. God is in the business of restoration. He takes down strongholds by working deeply and gently within us. He restores, redeems, and brings the freedom needed for the glorious life we were designed to live with Him. However, God does not work against our free will. Each of us must choose to let God redeem us. When I did, I was set free.

Most days I feel loved for who I am and free to be myself—not for my projection of who I think others want me to be and not for the things I have done, but for the real me, with all my faults. It is freeing to live this way. And although I am not yet perfect in walking in this freedom and do not expect to achieve perfection this side of heaven, I have the tools to win the strategic battles the Enemy uses to try and bring me down again. I often win those battles now, and it feels amazing!

This newfound freedom gave me courage to follow God's call to help set others free. I yearn to see others know they are loved and free in Christ. I want them to learn to overcome the Enemy. I see it now with the new eyes God has given me.

The war on our identities rages all around. I see brokenness in those who were raised in the American dream ideology. The new generation bucks it, proud to be different, and still comes up short. The depression and suicide rate climb higher each year, and mass shootings have become the norm. I recognize these as strategic battles for our identities.

The Enemy wages war to keep us from knowing our core identities as God's dearly loved children, created for a purpose and equipped to walk in it. The creator of the universe has a specific plan for each of us. This is what our souls have always searched for.

I pray that my journey becomes your inspiration to embark on your own journey to freedom. Each step of this book will include a piece of the story God used to rebuild my identity and reveal my purpose and will also provide some tools to assist with this ongoing battle.

Each chapter will include space to reflect on your story, a Bible study called "Learning Love," and a freedom application called "Finding Freedom." This will help you rebuild your identity, establish God's plan for your life, and build the armor you'll need to walk forward. In God's Word, we learn the truth of His love for us and how that sets us free. It is for freedom that Christ set us free (Galatians 5:1). The freedom to be fully loved and fully free is a freedom worth dying for. That is why He died for us.

I am so excited that you are ready to take the next step toward an amazing journey to a deeper relationship with your Creator. I am praying for you. Praying for healing and restoration. Praying for you to see the beauty in your created self, because God loves you. Most of all, I am praying for your newfound freedom. The freedom to be you, to do the great things God has called you to do, and to overcome the Enemy. I think a world of free overcomers, living in God's original design, would be a cool place to live.

Remember, no matter where you are, you are loved. You could not be more loved than you already are. I pray this journey helps you instill this truth deep in your soul. Amen.

AN ENCOUNTER WITH JESUS

*You intended to harm me, but God intended it all for
good. He brought me to this position so I could save the
lives of many people.*
Genesis 50:20 NLT

SOMETHING OMINOUS SIZZLED in the air.

My boss asked me to chat with him ten minutes before our
lunch break ended at our annual sales kickoff meeting in Denver.

My heart raced as I followed Robert to a quiet spot, away from
the hundreds of coworkers milling about. I had no idea what he
wanted, but something did not feel right. I knew him well enough
to notice the trepidation in his demeanor.

"Now, Micah," he began, cutting his eyes away from me. "You
know I need to do some layering to resolve the fact that I have
fourteen direct reports."

I nodded, my hopes rising. Maybe I'd been wrong about the

bad vibe. Instead, maybe this was it, and I was finally going to get the official promotion I had been struggling to gain for three years. Just a few months ago, at my midyear review, Robert had agreed that I was ready for this next step in my career.

He hesitated. I held my breath.

"We have decided to merge your division with Justin's. From now on, you'll report to him."

I continued to listen, with my thoughts racing. *Wait, what? I must have misunderstood. Justin is my peer, with less experience. How does that make sense?*

He continued, "This is only for a few months while we test the organizational theory in the partner sales division." Apparently seeing confusion and hurt flash in my eyes, he added a disclaimer. "Everything will change again in November."

Robert said it as though those facts defended the demotion he'd just handed me.

Suddenly, everything blurred as disillusionment took over. It was as though I was watching a movie instead of sitting right there with him. He continued talking, although I'm not sure what he said, and I don't even know how I responded.

I remember trying desperately to come back into the present, to think of the right questions to ask. But I couldn't find the words. It took all of me just to hold back tears. I did not want to cry in front of him, even though this was the most devastating news I had received in my career. And the opposite of what I had expected.

I wanted to give in to my anger and shout, "No way am I taking this!" I wanted to tell him he was a liar and remind him of all his positive comments on my performance review just a few months earlier. I wanted to shake him and make him remember that I, officially still a sales manager, had performed all the duties of both director and manager for the past three years and that he'd promised I was on the fast track to a promotion to director. That I put in an average of sixty hours a week to keep up with these two roles, which he should have filled with two people. That I had traveled to Denver every other week for meetings with the big shots, despite the hardship this caused for my family.

I should have told him I was doing everything he'd told me I had to do for the promotion. He'd never hinted at the danger of not receiving the official promotion to director—I was instead being demoted back to a sales manager, reporting to a sales director. A sales director who'd been my peer until a few seconds ago.

Then a worse thought hit me. Did I deserve the promotion?

Worse, did I deserve the demotion?

Shame whispered to me of all the things I had done wrong, like the HR issue with that tough employee last fall. Shame also reminded me that, despite my best efforts, our team ended the year 10 percent shy of the financial target. And shame suggested that maybe I wasn't cut out for the director role. Maybe the demotion was for the best. Maybe I still wasn't good enough, despite all those years of striving.

I have never been good enough.

Shame turned to acceptance as I realized I had no options. We were at our annual sales kickoff conference, and I was scheduled to present to thirty people in five minutes. I could not walk out. My flight did not leave until Monday, I was three hundred miles from home, and I was expected to attend the evening party. Besides, I needed this job. I was the only one keeping our family afloat financially, since my husband had just launched his own business. We needed the health benefits for us and our three children and the steady income that came from my corporate job.

My job was my whole career. It was everything I had been working for the last ten years. I had put my hope in this promotion. It was woven into my life's goals, my prayer life, our family's future. What would I do without this job? It had become my identity, and now I was confused about everything—even about who I was.

So I nodded in anguished agreement and reminded him I had to go to the next session, as though nothing was the matter at all.

I made it through the presentation and party, pushing away thoughts as they bubbled up, but sleep barely came that night. My thoughts overrode sleep as they churned with indignation at my boss, shame at myself, and anger at God. I'd thought God had called me to this job, but now I was not so sure.

Exhausted and still undone the next morning, I decided to leave the conference early and spend that Sunday wrestling through some things with God at the hotel near our Denver office. I had originally intended to head there in the early afternoon after the conference ended. I worried a bit that someone would notice I was not at the morning session, but I could no longer bring myself to attend.

I left in an Uber and headed to the hotel in the Denver Tech Center across the street from our Denver office. I felt so angry at God that I wanted to denounce Him yet so desperately lost that I knew I needed Him. When I arrived at the hotel, I tried to eat and sleep and even pray, but the anger, fueled by my deep hurt, consumed me. It filled me with an anxious rage that had me shaking.

Finally, I gave in to fury and hurled my pillow at the bed over and over while screaming at God. "How could you do this to me? How could you let this happen? I thought I was on the right path," I yelled, catapulting the pillow and connecting with the bed. I did this until I'd expended the last of my frantic energy. Then I collapsed on the floor in sobs.

This is when Jesus entered the room. I could feel His presence surround me, and I did not feel alone for the first time since the demotion experience nearly twenty-four hours ago. I sensed Him asking me to go for a walk. I put on my tennis shoes, hat, and sunglasses and headed to the park across the street. I started down a winding path on a chilly, sunny Colorado February morning.

I cried as I walked, but this time I let my true feelings bleed out to God. In my surrender, God revealed to me the chains keeping me in a quest for approval. God revealed to me that I had bound myself up in those chains, and they were killing my soul. I knew this was the truth, even though it was tough to face. I could feel God's amazing grace toward me as tears of release streamed down my cheeks. My heart was broken, but I knew He had allowed me to walk through the demotion because He wanted better for me.

It would be a few more days before I would fully grasp God's whole plan for the demotion, but I knew He was doing something good. I knew I had just en-countered my Savior, and I should hang on for dear life.

You intended to harm me, but God intended it all for good.
Gen 50:20

Looking back, I see God's goodness and how He unfolded His better plan for me through the demotion. God had tried other ways of showing me how off His course I was, like my Bible study book about seeking approval, but I am spiritually hard of hearing sometimes. God had to let me break before He could show me how far I had wandered from Him and His plan for me. God is so good to us, even when it hurts.

In fact, God is so good, He can take the bad we, or others, bring on ourselves and use it for our redemption and restoration.

Reflect: My self-worth and identity laid in the world's standard of success. I needed to climb the ladder at work, raise my kids well, and keep my ap-

I am not what I do.

pearance in perfect shape, or I didn't feel valuable. I thought if I worked hard enough, I could overcome the sense of *less than* that had penetrated my heart. But I never felt good enough, no matter how hard I tried. Then God sent me a Savior.

What pieces of my story remind you of your own?

_____

_____

_____

_____

_____

What or who do you rely on to give you value and to give your life significance?

_____

_____

_____

_____

_____

In what areas of your life do you currently strive to be good enough?

_____

_____

_____

_____

_____

Learning Love: The Woman at the Well

Then Jesus told her, "I am the Messiah!"
John 4:26 NLT

Change starts with an encounter with the Savior.

We see it over and over in Scripture. When God shows up, things change and, luckily for us, God comes to save us. For me, God showed up in a hard way, but it was not really a surprise visit. I had been asking Him for change. I'd had a different view of what that should look like (not a painful demotion), but God heard me and answered my prayer. So we will kick off this journey by allowing God to show up radically in our lives with truth.

Read from John about Jesus's interaction with the Samaritan woman at the well.

> To get there, he had to pass through Samaria. He came into Sychar, a Samaritan village that bordered the field Jacob had given his son Joseph. Jacob's well was still there. Jesus, worn out by the trip, sat down at the well. It was noon.
>
> A woman, a Samaritan, came to draw water. Jesus said, "Would you give me a drink of water?" (His disciples had gone to the village to buy food for lunch.)
>
> The Samaritan woman, taken aback, asked, "How come you, a Jew, are asking me, a Samaritan woman, for

a drink?" (Jews in those days wouldn't be caught dead talking to Samaritans.)

Jesus answered, "If you knew the generosity of God and who I am, you would be asking me for a drink, and I would give you fresh, living water."

The woman said, "Sir, you don't even have a bucket to draw with, and this well is deep. So how are you going to get this 'living water'? Are you a better man than our ancestor Jacob, who dug this well and drank from it, he and his sons and livestock, and passed it down to us?"

Jesus said, "Everyone who drinks this water will get thirsty again and again. Anyone who drinks the water I give will never thirst—not ever. The water I give will be an artesian spring within, gushing fountains of endless life."

The woman said, "Sir, give me this water so I won't ever get thirsty, won't ever have to come back to this well again!"

He said, "Go call your husband and then come back."

I have no husband," she said.

"That's nicely put: 'I have no husband.' You've had five husbands, and the man you're living with now isn't even your husband. You spoke the truth there, sure enough."

"Oh, so you're a prophet! Well, tell me this: Our ancestors worshiped God at this mountain, but you Jews insist that Jerusalem is the only place for worship, right?"

"Believe me, woman, the time is coming when you Samaritans will worship the Father neither here at this mountain nor there in Jerusalem. You worship guessing in the dark; we Jews worship in the clear light of day. God's way of salvation is made available through the

Jews. But the time is coming—it has, in fact, come—when what you're called will not matter and where you go to worship will not matter.

"It's who you are and the way you live that count before God. Your worship must engage your spirit in the pursuit of truth. That's the kind of people the Father is out looking for: those who are simply and honestly themselves before him in their worship. God is sheer being itself—Spirit. Those who worship him must do it out of their very being, their spirits, their true selves, in adoration."

The woman said, "I don't know about that. I do know that the Messiah is coming. When he arrives, we'll get the whole story."

"I am he," said Jesus. "You don't have to wait any longer or look any further." (John 4:4–26 MSG)

The woman at the well is me. She is all of us. She is hurting, ashamed both by the stigma she has endured from the world and the choices she made in her pain. She still lives in the sin of being chained to false beliefs and the bitterness that comes from living a lie. But God saw her and loved her. He would not allow her to stay that way, so He sent his Son to save her. In fact, the text reads that Jesus had to go to Samaria (John 4:4). We know the reason He "had to" was not because there was no other way to get where He was going but because the Father had compelled Him to go and save one of His beloved daughters. The Father could see her and wanted better for her. Jesus went because He wanted to meet with her and put her on a new path, leading her back to the goodness God had planned for her.

This is my story. This is your story. It is the heart of God for his beloved daughters. So let's dig in.

Read John 4:9 (MSG) again. "The Samaritan woman, taken aback, asked, 'How come you, a Jew, are asking me, a Samaritan woman, for a drink?' (Jews in those days wouldn't be dead talking to Samaritans.)"

Because the woman was a Samaritan, she was called a half-breed and considered an outcast by the religious leaders and other prideful people. According to her society, she was born not good enough. This is why Jesus's words took her aback. As the text says, Jews did not talk to Samaritans.

When Jesus points out her sinful lifestyle, she mentions the unfairness of her situation as a deflection. Listen to what she says in John 4:19–20 (MSG): "Oh, so you're a prophet! Well, tell me this: Our ancestors worshiped God at this mountain, but you Jews insist that Jerusalem is the only place for worship, right?"

I know I have asked Jesus such questions: "Why did You make me the chubby kid, Lord? I eat the same food as they do. I get the same amount of PE time, but they are not chubby. All I want is to fit in, but You made me different, and they torment me about it daily. In my head, I know they are the ones who are wrong, but in my heart, all I want is to be accepted. To feel good enough as I am."

Then we see that in her pain she made bad choices, trying to fill the void of not measuring up. But her poor choices only furthered her exile from society. Five husbands, and now with a man who was not even her husband, but none of them could fill the nagging in her soul telling her she was created for more. They couldn't erase the deep knowledge that she was not a mistake or an outcast.

She even had to hide from her own people. She went to the well at noon because everyone else went in the mornings, before the heat of the day. She found a way to get the water she needed while escaping the sneers of the respectable ladies.

We hide from our people in all kinds of ways. My successful-businesswoman facade hid the fact that I never felt good enough. I kept even my closest people at an arm's distance so they would not see the truth. I tried to prove I was good enough by working harder and longer than anyone else while secretly resenting each moment.

My disguise was my carefully crafted business attire, always one step more professional than our business-casual dress code required. Plus, I always came in early and stayed late to prove I could handle anything. I consistently projected the persona of confident leader, dutiful mother, and faithful Christian who always did everything right, while my insides told me I was not enough.

Just like the woman at the well, I formed a lifestyle that let me avoid the truth. And like the woman, I was bitter. I pretended I was fine. But whenever I made a mistake, my extreme shame and anger boiled up in a second, and I always ended up shouting at my poor husband and children. A quick temper is a sure sign of a broken and bitter heart.

But then Jesus showed up and changed everything. Listen to what Jesus said after He gently and lovingly pointed out the woman's sin.

> "I am he," said Jesus. "You don't have to wait any longer or look any further." (John 4:26 MSG)

Now picture yourself as the Samaritan woman hiding from your shame. But suddenly someone discovers the real you. It is God, and He has exposed all your insides, all the shame—everything you have been hiding. He knows it all. But instead of the judgement and condemnation you expect, God says, "It's all right, child. I have what you need, and I have come to save you. I have what you have always searched for: living water. There is no shame or fear here. There is only love. I am He, your Savior, the One who loves you. You do not have to hide anymore. I know all of you, all of what you have done, all the lies you believe, and I love you anyway. Will you let Me love you? Will you come with Me now and be free?"

We are saved when Jesus shows up and we decide to follow Him and ask for forgiveness. We are forgiven in an instant, and the Savior who died for us covers all our sin. Love abounds, and in love there is truth—truth that changes our hearts and our ways when we encounter it. Jesus tells the woman, "But the time is coming, indeed it is here now, when true worshippers will worship the Father in spirit and truth. The Father is looking for those who will worship him in that way" (John 4:23). Jesus tells her that regardless of what she has been through or has been told, God came looking for her so He could change her heart and she could follow Him.

After my encounter with Jesus, I realized I needed a heart change—a full on heart restoration. Although the demotion experience opened my eyes to the truth of how I had been living, it was not enough to help me stop believing the lies I had embraced for thirty-something years. It all sounded good, but on a deeper level, I did not believe God loved me as I was.

I needed to go deeper with my Savior. I needed to face the brokenness that manifested itself in my thoughts and feelings. I needed to sit on my Father's lap, expose my shame, and let Him mend the broken places I had been trying to hide, even from Him. I needed to *know* I was fully loved; not just told I was fully loved.

Finding Freedom: Be Found by the Savior

Release: Please answer the following questions in the space provided.

What lies has your culture or experiences told you about yourself?

_____

_____

_____

_____

Have you struggled with believing a truth that your head understands but your heart doesn't?

_____

_____

_____

_____

In what area do you need the Savior to find you?

_____

_____

_____

_____

Fly: The first step to heart transformation is allowing God to show you the lies you believe about yourself and allowing yourself to be saved. Start by laying it all out there for God and asking Him to meet you here. In the space below, pour out all the rejection you have experienced. Write down all the things you think about yourself but wish you did not. God knows anyway. It is time to stop hiding from Him and instead be found by the Savior.

Encouragement: Jesus is always ready to give you the living water that will help you to live free. "Anyone who is thirsty may come and drink! For the Scriptures declare, 'Rivers of living water will flow from his heart'" (John 7:38 NLT).

Let's Pray: "Search me, O God, and know my heart; test me and know my anxious thoughts. Point out anything in me that offends you, and lead me along the path of everlasting life" (Psalm 139:23–24 NLT).

Write your own prayer here:

_____

_____

_____

_____

_____

_____

_____

_____

_____

_____

EYES WIDE OPEN

A final word: Be strong in the Lord and His mighty
power. Put on all of God's armor so that you will be able
to stand firm against all strategies of the devil. For we are
not fighting against flesh-and-blood enemies, but against
evil rulers and authorities of the unseen world, against
mighty powers in this dark world, and against evil spirits
in the heavenly places.

Ephesians 6:9–10 NLT

MY SHAME RAGED AS I wrestled with God through my pain in the days following the demotion. Something inside me kept murmuring that God was seriously disappointed in me. This thought overwhelmed me, and I soon believed it. I was ashamed of myself and ashamed that I had made the promotion into an idol. I convinced myself that I deserved the pain of the demotion and that I deserved the tough love I thought God was giving me because of my sinfulness.

This belief only made my shame worse. I felt foolish for the way I had bought into my culture's lies. I berated myself because I should have known better. On top of getting demoted, I had failed God too, and now He was going to let me walk in my consequences.

But God was still working through my shame-filled days. At one of my lowest points, He arranged for me to visit my sister-in-law. She is a wise follower of Jesus who listens and counsels well. I shared everything that evening. For three hours, I tearfully poured out my bleeding heart and grave questions about God and His goodness toward me. And she picked up on something I did not even know I was doing. She said, "Micah, God does not correct us in shame."

Suddenly, I saw the war for my soul raging around me. I felt as if blinders fell off, and I hadn't even known I was wearing them. I could see the lies I believed about myself and about God. Losing them widened my view to a whole new perspective.

At some point during the last year, I had started believing God was leading me to the promotion. Getting it would mean I was finally good enough. The promotion had become my god, and I was striving to earn its favor.

My obsession with getting promoted had begun after attending a women's business conference. After listening to a powerful speaker, God spoke to me that He was calling me to lead, speak, and encourage other women. In a frenzy of energy that renewed purpose brings, I even told my pastor about my newfound vision. This vision was true, and it is still true. But the Enemy did not like the fact that I knew where God was calling me and that I was energized to get going. So he twisted the good things I believed into a very convincing lie. He whispered to my heart that I needed to be a senior leader at my company before I would be powerful and respected enough to start my calling of leading and speaking.

I believed I needed a promotion if God had called me. I even believed that if God loved me and wanted to bless me, He would get me promoted. He would help me become good enough to be promoted, which I wanted. I have always wanted to feel good enough and purposeful. So I bought the lie, blinded by the two things my damaged heart feared the most: that I was not good enough and that God was not good to me.

When the promotion did not happen, I believed it was because I had let God down and that He wanted me to continue striving to become better. In my humiliation, I believed God was letting me walk through this shame to teach me a lesson. The world had judged me and found me lacking again and again, and now I thought God measured me the same way.

Not so coincidentally, this sounds a lot like the twisted truth the Enemy served to Adam and Eve to get them to eat the forbidden fruit. Listen to the way the devil tricks them. First, he asks a question about the truth God told them, but he twists it a bit: "Did God really say you must not eat the fruit from any of the trees in the garden?" (Genesis 3:1 NIV). Then he twists the truth even further, using something the woman desires. He makes the woman question God's goodness toward her. "'You won't die!' the serpent replied to the woman. 'God knows that your eyes will be opened as soon as you eat it, and you will be like God, knowing both good and evil'" (Genesis 3:4–5). And just like me "the woman was convinced" (Genesis 3:6).

This is spiritual warfare.

We must understand we are in a battle. If we weren't, we wouldn't need armor. But we don't fight this battle with flesh and blood, but rather in the Spirit world (Ephesians 6:10). We are spirit beings as well as physical beings. Often our hardest wars rage in our souls rather than in the physical realm. Our Enemy is also a spiritual being. He wants nothing more than to lead us into his trap

Look, I have given you authority over all the power of the enemy, and you can walk among snakes and scorpions and crush them. Nothing will injure you.
Luke 10:19

31

and away from God. This is the epic battle we fight as we walk in the physical realm.

But before we get discouraged about this battle, we need to remember that it is already won. From the first moment after Adam and Eve's fall into sin, God set a plan in place that would overcome death. Throughout all generations, God's plan has been to save us from the brutal tyranny of sin and death (Romans 8:2). God is gracious to us, even in our disobedience. He loves us and guides us away from the sin that destroys us, even when we believe lies about Him.

I fell into our culture's beliefs that God has standards that I needed to meet in order to be good enough. I assumed He was a hard-nosed taskmaster because, in my own fear and shame about myself, I wanted to prove myself worthy of love. I wanted standards I could meet so I could finally feel worthy. But because I could not measure up, I believed I was not good enough in God's eyes. But with my eyes wide open, crying at the dinner table with my sister-in-law, I saw the truth about God. I understood that His grace and love toward me do not fail. That night I discovered a life-altering truth about God: He doesn't base His love on what we do but rather on who He is, and He is love.

Reflect: Write your answers in the spaces provided below.

I am a warrior.

Because of lies from our culture and the Enemy, I had a wrong view of who God is and how He thinks of me. Satan used those lies to keep me from God. It's hard to remember that we are in a battle for our souls. But we are, and our Enemy is conniving. We must see the battle and the devil's tactics if we are to recognize our lies and win the war.

What do you believe about God's character?

_____

_____

_____

_____

_____

How do you think God thinks of you and acts toward you?

_____

_____

_____

_____

_____

Have you ever thought about spiritual warfare? Did you realize that the Enemy lies to you about who God is and who you are because he wants to keep you away from God?

_____

_____

_____

_____

_____

Learning Love: God Comes into the Garden

*When they heard the sound of God strolling in the garden
in the evening breeze, the Man and his Wife hid in the
trees of the garden, hid from God.*
Genesis 3:8 MSG

Our Enemy is deceptive in his mission, and one of his best tactics is to make us think God could not possibly be good and that He is frequently mad at us. The Enemy gets us to sin by using deception. Then he uses our shame to make us believe God is angry, driving us further from the God who wants to gather us close and wash us clean. This is a successful tactic because it has a cyclical effect. When we don't trust God, we don't follow God. Instead we follow our flesh or the lies Satan whispers to us. When we follow these lies, we feel shame as the natural consequence. Then the Enemy lies to us again, saying God is terribly angry with us.

We separate ourselves from God when we think He is mad at us. Then hopelessness sets in and we sin even more, trying to fill the void. And on and on until we cannot find the glorious life God intended us to have.

It is an ugly cycle, for sure. But God, in His amazing grace, saw this and rescued us at the onset. The moment He met Adam and Eve in the garden, He put the plan in place to rescue them from their own wrongdoing. And He does this every time He meets with us now. This is the heart of our loving and gracious God.

Before we move on in this journey, we must also identify what we believe about God. We must see what lies the Enemy and our shame-filled hearts have told us about our loving God. Then we need to learn who He is and what He thinks of us.

Read this passage from Genesis and look for the way God reacts to Adam and Eve's sin.

> The serpent was clever, more clever than any wild animal God had made. He spoke to the Woman: "Do I understand that God told you not to eat from any tree in the garden?"
>
> The Woman said to the serpent, "Not at all. We can eat from the trees in the garden. It's only about the tree in the middle of the garden that God said, 'Don't eat from it; don't even touch it or you'll die.'"
>
> The serpent told the Woman, "You won't die. God knows that the moment you eat from that tree, you'll see what's really going on. You'll be just like God, knowing everything, ranging all the way from good to evil."
>
> When the Woman saw that the tree looked like good eating and realized what she would get out of it— she'd know everything!—she took and ate the fruit and then gave some to her husband, and he ate.
>
> Immediately the two of them did "see what's really going on"—saw themselves naked! They sewed fig leaves together as makeshift clothes for themselves.
>
> When they heard the sound of God strolling in the garden in the evening breeze, the Man and his Wife hid in the trees of the garden, hid from God.
>
> God called to the Man: "Where are you?"
>
> He said, "I heard you in the garden and I was afraid because I was naked. And I hid."
>
> God said, "Who told you you were naked? Did you eat from that tree I told you not to eat from?"

The Man said, "The Woman you gave me as a companion, she gave me fruit from the tree, and, yes, I ate it."

God said to the Woman, "What is this that you've done?"

"The serpent seduced me," she said, "and I ate." (Genesis 3:1–13 MSG)

In Genesis 3:8 we see God coming into the garden in the cool evening, strolling leisurely. But Adam and Eve hide. Notice the time of day and His pace. He does not come rushing in, furious and scolding with a mighty force. This helps us get a grasp of who God is and how He acts toward us, even in our disobedience.

Think about yourself. Let's say someone did something very wrong toward you. Perhaps you told them not to do something, but they did it anyway. Would you wait and cool off before confronting them? Would you walk leisurely toward them? I probably would not. I would run to them in the heat of the moment and let them have it! However this is not who God is. He is gracious and kind, slow to anger and rich in love (Psalm 145:8).

Adam and Eve hid themselves from God in their shame. As with all humans after them, our own shame accuses us, and we project that onto other people, thinking they are against us. We think God is against us for this same reason, and so did Adam and Eve. However God is not like us. We need to be careful not to make God into what our shame tells us about Him. He does not treat us as our sins deserve (Psalm 103:10).

Most important of all, before God passes judgement on Adam and Eve, He puts a plan into motion to save them. This is the heart of our God. He is Savior and Redeemer first, desiring above all else to have His children with Him. Then He is just, requiring justice and consequences for wrong actions. Our God is both gracious and just in exactly the right measure.

God is love and loves us more than we deserve. The Enemy does not want us to know this, though, because it frees us. We must constantly grow in our knowledge of God so we can reject the lies of the Enemy. It is vital to our relationship with God that we know who He is and what He thinks of us.

Finding Freedom: Know God and the Enemy

Release: Do my thoughts toward God and myself line up with the biblical description of God: gracious, compassionate, slow to anger, and abounding in love?

_____

_____

_____

_____

_____

_____

_____

_____

_____

How would my life change if I believed God understood me and was compassionate toward me, even in my fallen state? What would change if I believed that instead of being disappointed in me, God desired to redeem me?

_____

_____

_____

_____

_____

_____

_____

How would I view shameful events in my life if I saw them as the work of the Enemy to make me believe wrongly about God and myself?

_____

_____

_____

_____

_____

_____

Fly: We can get so lost in this physical reality that we can't see the spiritual warfare around us. The Enemy is a deceiver. His lies are so convincing we cannot see them on our own. Find another believer, a pastor, or a Christian counselor, and talk openly to them about your situation or beliefs about God. Let them know your thoughts about yourself and what you think God thinks of you. Ask them to help you discover any lies you may believe about God. Then, either by yourself or with your friend, review a painful memory and pinpoint the lies the Enemy told you. See how God remained faithful to His character and waited for you.

Encouragement: God is mysterious, and His ways are higher than our ways. But we can grow in our knowledge of Him as we continue in a relationship with Him. Peter wrote, "Rather, you must grow in the grace and knowledge of our Lord and Savior Jesus Christ" (2 Peter 3:18 NLT). God is gracious to us as we learn about Him and learn to trust Him more. And we will continue to learn that His love never fails (Psalm 136:1).

Let's Pray: *Father*, You are good and desire good for us, but we have an Enemy who lies to us to keep us from believing this. Please help us recognize the lies we believe about You and ourselves as we grow in our knowledge of You. Thank You for Your constant grace and never-ending love. In Jesus's name, amen.

Write your own prayer here:

CHOOSING THE JOURNEY

*And this is the plan: At the right time he will bring every-
thing together under the authority of Christ—everything
in heaven and on earth.*

Ephesians 1:10 NLT

WITH MY NEW UNDERSTANDING OF God and His posture toward me,
I had a gut-wrenching choice to make. You see, I knew God
wanted me to stay in the sales manager position at the organization
that had just demoted me, but I kept vacillating between forgiveness and outrage at the unfairness of it all. Some days, I looked
for another job. My husband and I even discussed picking up and
moving our family to a different state. Other days, I went to work
and let it all go, having fun with the project I was working on. Even
though I knew in my heart what God wanted for me, my feelings
kept me in limbo.

And although I wanted to leave the limbo, resentment kept
boiling to the surface. I was not truly healed from finding my
worth in the approval of man and was having a hard time forgiving

those who'd rejected me and made me feel worthless. I felt they owed me the promotion to director because of all my hard work. Forgiving them would be letting them win. Despite knowing God was working on something bigger than I could see in the moment, my heart was wrapped in bitterness.

Regardless of my feelings, however, it was abundantly clear that God wanted me to stay where I was for now. I knew the journey to freedom was not about this circumstance, but rather it involved letting Him lead me wherever He wanted in this season. Full surrender kept eluding me though because I was afraid to let go of the resentment.

After a few weeks of wrestling with bitterness, I sensed God waking me up at four o'clock in the morning to speak to me. I have a love-hate relationship with God's ability to wake me from sleep. I love that He answered my pleading prayers the night before, but I disliked waking up so early.

He began to teach me with the following vision.

Imagine that I am a traveler sitting in my vehicle at the entrance to a narrow, single-track path. I know this path leads to the promised land. I want to go, but I'm pulling a trailer. It has two wheels and is wide for stability. The trailer is filled with all the things I've picked up throughout my life. It has plaques of resentment I made because I didn't want to forget offenses. It has bricks of rejection and shame, which I used to build a wall around my broken heart. It also holds stones of judgement, which I have used to shame others. It has all my idols: the heavy, little statues of title, performance, perfection, and the approval of others, which I have crafted to worship. It also has the heavy—oh, so heavy—mirror of comparison I use to compare myself to others. Oh yes, this trailer is very wide. Too wide for this path.

The only things I can take with me on this path are the things I need. The bread of life that sustains me. The water that never runs dry. The breath of life breathed into me. The gifts God has given me, including just the measure of faith I will need for every next step. These are the only things I can carry on this path. There is no room for any of the stuff in the trailer.

I have to trust God enough to choose.

As you can imagine, this answer brought me to tears. Even as I wrote it, I knew the Spirit had poured out the answer I had been seeking. I wanted it to be my way, but God had a different way in mind. I didn't know then that many months later, He would give me something much better than a mere promotion. This gift from God would bring back the dreams I had when I was a little girl and would allow me to believe again that they were possible.

I decided that day to stop vacillating between whether to stay or go at work. Instead I would trust God. I forgave my superiors and moved forward with the project that awaited my attention. But most of all, I decided that neither the promo-

Jesus replied, "I am the bread of life. Whoever comes to me will never be hungry again. Whoever believes in me will never be thirsty. John 6:35

tion nor demotion said anything about who I was or my value. I chose to take the journey and recover my identity with God alone. The first step was to let go of the past—all the resentment and rejection—and wait for God to show me the next step after that.

Sometimes God asks us to trust that He has a better way. He knows our hearts better than we do, and He knows what our hearts cry out for. God sees into the broken places of our hearts, which we have long ago hidden away in an attempt at self-preservation. He desires to heal our hearts because freedom is found in full redemption. However He is not a forceful God. He gives us free will, and with this freedom, we get the choice to follow Him or not. We get the choice to allow wounded places to heal or not. The first step is choosing to follow.

Reflect: God had a plan that I was not sure I wanted. I had to choose to believe His plan was the path toward the life I wanted, and it was better than I could have imagined for myself.

I am free to choose

Has God asked you to do something, but you hesitate to obey because you're not sure you want to go that way? What about God's way scares you?

_____

_____

_____

_____

_____

_____

What in your trailer is weighing you down and keeping you from the path you were created to walk?

_____

_____

_____

_____

_____

_____

Learning Love: Get Off Your Mat and Walk

Jesus told him, "Stand up, pick up your mat, and walk!"
John 5:8 NLT

God always wants us to be healed, but He doesn't always do it the way we want. Even before the demotion, I wanted to be healed. For months, I had known something was vitally wrong. I was burned out, weary, and felt like a victim of my circumstances. This was not the best side of me.

Looking back at my journal entries from those months, I see that I prayed for healing. I knew I had an idol and prayed to release it. So why did the demotion experience flabbergast me? I wanted God to fix it my way. I thought I knew what God should do to heal me. I wanted to get the promotion and also have God somehow heal me.

He had a better plan.

We see this same story in one of Jesus's miraculous healing stories in John.

> Some time later, Jesus went up to Jerusalem for one of the Jewish festivals. Now there is in Jerusalem near the Sheep Gate a pool, which in Aramaic is called Bethesda[a] and which is surrounded by five covered colonnades. Here a great number of disabled people used to lie—the

blind, the lame, the paralyzed. One who was there had been an invalid for thirty-eight years. When Jesus saw him lying there and learned that he had been in this condition for a long time, he asked him, "Do you want to get well?"

"Sir," the invalid replied, "I have no one to help me into the pool when the water is stirred. While I am trying to get in, someone else goes down ahead of me."

Then Jesus said to him, "Get up! Pick up your mat and walk." At once the man was cured; he picked up his mat and walked.

The day on which this took place was a Sabbath. (John 1:5–9 NIV)

The man who needed healing believed he would receive it only if he was the first person in the pool when the angel stirred the waters. He sat at the pool for decades wanting to be healed this way. So when Jesus asked him if he wanted to be healed, he tells Jesus that he does not have any one to help him get into the pool. He had his mind set on this type of healing, but Jesus had a better way.

Jesus wanted to heal him by his faith, not his circumstances. When the man obeyed Jesus's command to get up and walk, he was healed.

Jesus had a totally different method in mind for this man's healing and also for my healing. Maybe He does for you too.

Finding Freedom: Go with God

Release: Do you have an expectation in mind for the manner in which you want God to perform your healing? Could He have a different plan?

_____

_____

_____

_____

Ask God to reveal the next step toward your healing. Write down what you hear Him say.

_____

_____

_____

_____

Write out on a note card what this could look like over the next few weeks.

Fly: This is the time to take the next step on your path toward healing and freedom. Make time this week to start making progress toward this step and to pray about it. Schedule time on your calendar to begin taking the next step. Put your note card somewhere where you will read it daily.

Encouragement: God's way is trustworthy, even if it seems odd or counterintuitive. Jesus healed with spit and sand, days after death, and on the Sabbath, which was very counterculture. Go with God's plan.

Let's Pray: *Father*, You are good and want to give us good things. Your Word tells us so. Your ways are higher than our ways, so sometimes we cannot understand. Help us to go with You when we are afraid or unsure of Your way. Give us the courage and shed light on good next steps. Thank You for Your guidance, Father. In Jesus's name, amen.

Write your own prayer here:

_____

_____

_____

_____

_____

_____

_____

_____

Section 2

JOURNEY TO THE HEART

He heals the brokenhearted and bandages their wounds
Psalm 147:3 NLT

THE PROBLEM WITH A BROKEN heart is that it needs to be tended, not disregarded, if we want it to work properly again. An unhealed heart is an easy trap for the Enemy to use against us. These are the crucial lessons God revealed to me on my journey to the center of my heart.

Before this journey, I didn't know moving forward meant going backward. But it did. To receive the healing I sought, I had to go back through layers of unhealed hurts. And I was not a fan of going backward. Especially to places I preferred to keep carefully tucked away, never to be visited again. I wanted to get over them and quickly move forward.

However my journey taught me a lot about the fragile human heart and how the Enemy uses it for his advantage. I know now that healing hearts is hard work that only our almighty healer can accomplish as we trust Him. He created our hearts for the perfection of the garden. Because of that, we are so taken aback by the brokenness of the world, we often don't know how to process our hurts, let alone heal from them. This means the Enemy can easily twist them.

Along my journey, I found old injuries—hurts I had never dealt with. These injuries had manifested themselves into lies, and Satan constantly threw them at me. I had not seen the connection between my actions (like trying to work for significance), the wounds that had cut deep in my younger years, and the lies playing on repeat.

But God led me back to them so He could heal me of them. I had to move back to go forward.

At age thirty-seven, I had not yet learned how to lean on the tender care of God to heal from wounds. Being the go-forward, run-fast, get-it-done person God made me, the slow grieving required for healing had always eluded me. And honestly, I wanted it to be easier. I wanted God to wave a magic wand and make my heart all better. That is simply not how it works though. Healing is a process. We work through our broken circumstances as we live in the new light and new life we have from Jesus.

I am not going to tell you the next steps were easy, but I can tell you they were worth it. I know God in all new ways now. I know Him as the faithful provider of my true needs. I know Him as the tender healer of my heart. The One who holds it while it fits itself back together and the One who grieves with me along the way. I know Him as the God who sees every moment of my life and each time my heart has been shattered by the brokenness of the world. And I know Him as the almighty Redeemer, whose love wins the battle. He is the One who can take our worst moments, shattered heart fragments, and tears and put them all back together again far more beautifully than before.

This is a God worth knowing.

And I know myself better too. I know my hardships have shaped me, both in good and bad ways. I know my natural tendencies, how I deal with things, and what to watch out for moving forward. I know the true me without all the armor I built to keep myself protected from the world's brokenness. And with this knowledge, I have more empathy for myself and less shame. It is hard to be mad at myself and berate myself when I realize how my wounds have affected me and that the Enemy reminds me of these things to keep me chained. I learned to be more patient with myself. I learned to allow for emotions and grieving, using my gift of time. Most importantly, I learned to give myself fewer expectations and become more dependent on God.

The best knowledge I gained through this part of my journey, however, was a good helping of the truth. God revealed the lies I believed about myself. I hadn't thought about some of those lies in years, long before I was follower of Jesus. The lies had become part of my normal existence, so I never questioned them. Seeing them again gave me a chance to reevaluate them through the eyes of God and His truths. The Bible states that knowing the truth sets us free (John 8:32), and I could not agree more. But to know the truth, I first had to uncover the lies.

This next section is all about discovering the lies so you can face them head on, tear them down with the truth of God, and be ready to rebuild. I am praying for you as you journey into your heart. I am praying that God's light shines in the dark places you have kept hidden. And I am praying that once the lies are exposed to the light of Christ, the darkness will flee. Amen.

FACING THE REAL FEAR

But Ruth replied, "Don't ask me to leave you and turn back. Wherever you go, I will go; wherever you live, I will live. Your people will be my people, and your God will be my God."
Ruth 1:16 NLT

A FEW MONTHS AFTER MY demotion, my husband and I did the hardest thing I have done in my life thus far. We dropped off our darling girl, nearly sixteen years old, to get the help we could no longer provide. We left her in the care of experts at a Christ-centered, intensive-therapy camp, with just the slightest glimmer of hope that God would be faithful and she would be healed from her mental distress.

She had suffered from anxiety, depression, and low self-worth for a few years. The issue had escalated until it was too large for us, first-time parents to a teenager, to handle alone. Prayerfully, we decided she needed some time away from her peers and her family.

Our small town did not have the resources to help her, so we were forced to look elsewhere, even outside our state. We decided on an intensive-therapy camp near the border of Wyoming and Montana, eight hundred miles from home.

We drove her there on the first day of summer break, knowing she would be there for at least eight weeks. As we drove away the following day, the pain of being away from my hurting girl, along with thoughts of fear and doubt, swirled in my mind and engulfed me. I was terrified we had made a mistake. Terrified that she would never get healed from this. Terrified that as her mom, I was the cause. Certainly, I must have done something wrong. Once again, I was not good enough.

I cried for a bit but mostly felt numb on our drive back to Denver. My husband (her adopted dad) and I tried to talk of other things to fill the time and cover the heartbreak.

And yet I decided, against the gnawing in my heart, that I could go to work in the Denver office the next day. Despite my anguish over my oldest child, my only girl, I could be strong for two more days until the weekend, because God forbid I should lose my job on top of everything else spiraling out of control in my life.

That decision quickly blew up in my face.

I hadn't told my boss about my daughter because I was afraid to show weakness. I also hadn't told him I would be out of the office the past two days. He was frustrated, and he had a right to be. But that didn't mean it didn't sting, when he asked where I had been and shared his frustration with me. I'd been afraid of admitting family hardship to the man who, just months ago, had proven he was better at his job than I was and had become my boss.

Throughout the day, my fear bubbled up as anger in some moments and as tears in others. I was a nervous wreck. I knew I should leave, but I was afraid to. I was ashamed of this situation. I thought it spoke to my unworthiness at parenting, at work, and at life in general. All the fear of failure with my daughter, failure at work, and failure in life coursed through my veins.

That evening I had dinner with my sister-in-law, the same dear friend who had given me wise counsel throughout this journey. We talked for hours as I laid out the hurt and the fear. First I described how it felt to fail at parenting, and then I rehashed the demotion. These two events felt connected to the constant failing, betrayal, and rejection that had always filled my life.

We talked about my confusion about God's involvement with these situations. Why had this new pain brought the bitterness from the demotion to the surface again? I'd been so sure I had forgiven my boss and given up my title idol months earlier. Why were these things connected? What was God asking me to do?

I cried. She listened. I wrestled. She listened. She closed in prayer and one very clear thought hit me. God told me to take the next week off to seek and pray and heal. He stated that I was not okay to go to work and that I did not need to be strong enough to work right now, even though I thought I needed to work. Instead, I needed to face the unhealed pain from my past and process my daughter's situation with Him, or I would never truly heal. And most of all, He said I needed to trust Him instead of thinking I had to be strong enough to go to work when facing such a hard family time.

For a person who has issues with idolizing work and a proving-my-worth-through-productivity identity, this request was truly frightening. It was like asking me to move to a new city with no friends, no family, and no job prospects. I had always worked through everything on my own, and God revealed to me that I did this because I was afraid not to. I derived my value through productivity and approval, especially in times like these when I felt worthless. Work was my chosen way of proving I was good enough. It was a shield to hide

Don't be afraid, for I am with you. Don't be discouraged, for I am your God. I will strengthen you and help you. I will hold you up with my victorious right hand.
Isaiah 41:10

my biggest fear: that I was not good enough and would someday be found out. I did not trust God enough to let go of the one thing that kept me running away from this fear. But that was exactly what He asked me to do.

That evening I told my husband about my instructions to take a break from work so I could heal. My husband agreed. He probably knew I needed it long before I did. He has always been so kind as I struggle through my pain. So I prepped myself to walk into work, face my boss, and admit that I was not okay, not strong enough, and needed the next week off. I had started to believe God was for me and was leading me to better places. Now I not only said I believed it, but I wanted to prove it with action.

I never would have faced the old, unhealed hurts in my heart or processed the new hurt with my daughter's situation if I'd kept pushing forward at work and running from the fear that I was not good enough. God knew that. God knows my heart so well. He knew that trying to work through a family emergency proved I was striving for value. So although He didn't reveal much about what this time off would look like, I walked into it hopeful that God was faithful as I followed Him into the unknown. I was frightened to the core, but I also had the slightest hopeful glimmer of a promised land flowing with love and freedom.

Reflect: God asked me to let go of work and go with Him through hard circumstances with my daughter be-cause it was a part of His redemptive

I am courageous

plan. He knew my real fear was being found unworthy. And He knew I was using work to run from the fear instead of facing the fear and healing.

What is the thing you most fear?

_____

_____

_____

_____

_____

_____

Is your fear interwoven with unhealed pain from past circumstances?

_____

_____

_____

_____

_____

_____

_____

Learning Love: Chesed Love

*When Naomi saw that Ruth was determined to go with
her, she said nothing more.*
Ruth 1:18 NLT

Learn about chesed love from the story of Ruth.

In the days when the judges ruled in Israel, a severe
famine came upon the land. So a man from Bethlehem
in Judah left his home and went to live in the country
of Moab, taking his wife and two sons with him. The
man's name was Elimelech, and his wife was Naomi.
Their two sons were Mahlon and Kilion. They were
Ephrathites from Bethlehem in the land of Judah. And
when they reached Moab, they settled there.

Then Elimelech died, and Naomi was left with her
two sons.

The two sons married Moabite women. One married a woman named Orpah, and the other a woman
named Ruth. But about ten years later, both Mahlon
and Kilion died. This left Naomi alone, without her two
sons or her husband.

Then Naomi heard in Moab that the Lord had

blessed his people in Judah by giving them good crops again. So Naomi and her daughters-in-law got ready to leave Moab to return to her homeland. With her two daughters-in-law she set out from the place where she had been living, and they took the road that would lead them back to Judah.

But on the way, Naomi said to her two daughters-in-law, "Go back to your mothers' homes. And may the Lord reward you for your kindness to your husbands and to me. May the Lord bless you with the security of another marriage." Then she kissed them good-bye, and they all broke down and wept.

"No," they said. "We want to go with you to your people."

But Naomi replied, "Why should you go on with me? Can I still give birth to other sons who could grow up to be your husbands? No, my daughters, return to your parents' homes, for I am too old to marry again. And even if it were possible, and I were to get married tonight and bear sons, then what? Would you wait for them to grow up and refuse to marry someone else? No, of course not, my daughters! Things are far more bitter for me than for you, because the Lord himself has raised his fist against me."

And again they wept together, and Orpah kissed her mother-in-law good-bye. But Ruth clung tightly to Naomi. "Look," Naomi said to her, "your sister-in-law has gone back to her people and to her gods. You should do the same."

But Ruth replied, "Don't ask me to leave you and turn back. Wherever you go, I will go; wherever you live, I will live. Your people will be my people, and your God will be my God. Wherever you die, I will die, and there I will be buried. May the Lord punish me severely if I allow anything but death to separate us!" When

Naomi saw that Ruth was determined to go with her, she said nothing more.

So the two of them continued on their journey. When they came to Bethlehem, the entire town was excited by their arrival. "Is it really Naomi?" the women asked.

"Don't call me Naomi," she responded. "Instead, call me Mara, for the Almighty has made life very bitter for me. I went away full, but the Lord has brought me home empty. Why call me Naomi when the Lord has caused me to suffer and the Almighty has sent such tragedy upon me?"

So Naomi returned from Moab, accompanied by her daughter-in-law Ruth, the young Moabite woman. They arrived in Bethlehem in late spring, at the beginning of the barley harvest. (Ruth 1:1–22)

The story of Ruth is about Naomi and Ruth's belief in God as a loyal redeemer and God proving to them that He is. Naomi and Ruth had both recently suffered tragedy—the kind none of us want. Naomi lost her husband and two sons and is now widowed in her old age. Ruth lost her husband, who was one of Naomi's sons, in her young age before having any children with him. Therefore Naomi tells Ruth to leave her and go back to her people and find a new husband, despite the fact that the two women had become close family.

Naomi views the tragic events as a sign that God has left her. She thinks she has become God's enemy somehow, and she is afraid. She wants Ruth to leave her and find a new life. Ruth, on the other hand, shows great faith in Yahweh, who is not even her people's God, by believing God can still redeem Naomi and Ruth's lives, despite their hard circumstances. Naomi wants to run from the hardships, but Ruth wants to face the fear and let God have His way.

Ruth chooses to stay with Naomi and follow her to Bethlehem, where she would be a widowed outsider without much hope for the future. Her choices and actions reveal her faith in God, and she becomes an example of God's loyal love to Naomi. God radically blesses Ruth for this faith, giving her Boaz as a husband. Through their marriage and childbearing, Ruth enters the lineage of Jesus.

The Hebrew word the Bible uses to portray Ruth's love for Naomi is *chesed*. Chesed means "the loyal love of God." It's never failing, always present through all things.

I would love to say that through the demotion experience and hard season with our daughter, I had faith like Ruth, but that would be dishonest. I was much more like Naomi, wanting to run from the fear and the hurt these hardships caused. I wanted to believe God was still for me, but fear of facing the pain had kept me running.

This is one of our tendencies as humans in hard times. We see the hard time as evidence that God is either not good, or we are not good and are not worthy of good. We become afraid. But just as Ruth did for Naomi, God came in and showed me His loyalty when I took the week off to heal with Him. I surrendered my constant running from the real fears and instead faced them head on. And even in my distrust, God was with me. He took care of the things I thought I needed to be strong for, letting me lay them down and spend time healing. He showed me His loyalty to my redemption and that He would go with me on this journey.

He showed me chesed love—the loyal love that never gives up and can redeem all things. Faith in His chesed love is all He requires.

Finding Freedom: Turn and Face the Fear

Release: Where do you run in times of hardship or when unhealed pain bubbles up to the surface?

_____

_____

_____

_____

Do you believe in God's chesed love and desire to redeem hard things in your life?

_____

_____

_____

_____

Fly: Write out some of the unhealed pain you know is in your heart and declare that you are not afraid of facing it anymore. Now plan some time with God. You do not have to take off a whole week as I did. Just plan some time to face the pain with God over the next few days. It could be half an hour in the morning or evening or over a weekend. He will be faithful to meet you there with His chesed love and the power to redeem.

Encouragement: "The Lord is close to the brokenhearted; he rescues those whose spirits are crushed" (Psalm 34:18).

Let's Pray: *Father*, we admit that facing the pain in our lives is hard. Thank You for understanding. Help us to overcome the fear and stop running so we can sit on Your lap and heal these wounds. In Jesus's name, amen.

Write your own prayer here:

_____

_____

_____

_____

_____

_____

_____

_____

_____

_____

_____

ILL-FITTING ARMOR

The Lord who rescued me from the claws of the lion and
the bear will rescue me from this Philistine!
1 Samuel 17:37 NLT

GOD MET ME AS SOON as I stopped running and turned to face the real fears in my heart. The first day of my week off, He started peeling back the layers of my poorly bandaged heart. Memories I'd tried to shove away came rushing back with far too much clarity. It was as if they had just happened, rather than sixteen and thirty years ago. I could feel the Holy Spirit nudging me to sit with God and address the hurtful experiences I feared facing most. With trepidation, I did.

The first morning of my week off, just three days after dropping off our daughter at therapy camp, I sat outside my little home office in a clearing surrounded by oak brush and pine. I let the Spirit lead me through the tough-girl facade I'd created long ago. God called me to get brutally honest with myself, but He held my hand so I was a little less afraid.

The truth poured out.

Everyone in my life knew me as strong and driven. I have nick-names at work that allude to strength and tenacity. 'A dog with a bone' was one of the most recent metaphor's someone used to describe me. I act strong all the time, even around my closest friends. My closest family members, who have often received my wrath, have called me coldhearted. Many of them think I stopped crying several years ago.

It was all an act of self-preservation. A defense mechanism. An armor I built to protect my broken and bleeding heart from the onslaught of pain that began a few months after my twenty-first birthday, sixteen years before the day I sat in the clearing with God.

And this performance of strength was often so convincing that I had bought into it as well. It had become my identity. It was so deeply ingrained in me, I never let my guard down, even with God. I wore my armor to the throne room because deep inside, I was afraid to take it off. Ever. I was terrified to face the pain.

But I could not heal from the pain if I did not face it. So God led me back to the frightful night when I built this ill-fitting armor for myself.

Sixteen years ago I faced a hardship no one should ever have to endure. I was twenty-one years old, and my beautiful blonde daughter, Hannah, had just been born. I was head over heels in love with her, but to make ends meet, I had to go back to work when she was just six-weeks old. Her biological father had a part-time job and went to mechanic school in the evening, so he was able to be her daytime caretaker.

One night, seven weeks into her little life, she cried inconsolably as I was trying to get her settled for bed. I tried to comfort her with food, rocking, singing—anything that had worked before. I thought maybe she was gassy, so I applied some pressure to her little tummy as my mom had shown me how to do. She was a tiny thing, so my hand reached across her tummy and her ribcage.

That's when I noticed a weird popping feeling near her ribs as she heaved in little sobs.

Looking back, I realize that I knew what it was, but I refused to believe it. I sat there holding her up against my shoulder, feeling the popping, and trying to figure out what to do. I finally settled on the grave truth that I had to take her to the ER.

After that, the details are a blur. This story is so painful that I think my brain has tried to file it away so I can't continually recall the trauma.

Her father met me at the hospital after I called him on the way to the ER. We went into the exam room together with Hannah after a long wait in the waiting room, and the doctor conducted a short examination. A police officer came to our room and escorted us and the doctor to the x-ray department.

They did not bring Hannah back to us after the x-ray. Instead the doctors questioned us without telling us the official diagnosis. After her father and I answered their questions, they informed us that Hannah had a couple of broken ribs and would be transferred to the children's hospital via ambulance. We could not go with her. We were to drive to the Social Services office somewhere in Denver.

I was terrified. Everything became a blur. I honestly cannot remember how we got to Child Protective Services or where it was located. By this time, it was well past midnight, and I had been up since five thirty in the morning after a broken night's sleep.

At the Social Services office, they interrogated me first. My pulse still races when I try to recall this memory. This was one of the scariest things I have ever been through. They played good cop-bad cop, first yelling at me and then speaking softly and encouragingly to me. They did everything in their power to try to break me. I did break down in tears. But I did not know what had happened. I choked back sobs as I told them for the hundredth time that I did not know how her little ribs had gotten broken.

They interrogated Hannah's biological dad second, as I sat in the waiting room with his mom. It took less than ten minutes for them to come out and tell us he had confessed to breaking her ribs. He said he was holding Hannah as she was screaming while he was trying to make her a bottle. He claimed he had almost dropped her and that he had accidentally squeezed too hard as he was catching her from falling. The social workers did not believe him, and neither did I, but that was the story he stuck to. They charged him with child abuse.

As they led me back to the interrogation room, another officer led him out in cuffs. They informed me that the state was pressing charges against him and that neither of us could have Hannah until the court decided what was best for her two days later. He was going to jail. Hannah was staying at the children's hospital for the night, and Grandma would pick her up the following day. Even though I was not charged with anything, she was now in the custody of the state. Until they decided I was not a party to the crime, she was not allowed to be with me. I was going home alone.

I cried myself to sleep that night. I shamed myself for all I had done wrong. How could I not have seen that her father was capable of such a cruel act? Did I not notice that he was overwhelmed with caring for an infant? Had I really married a child abuser?

I felt like a terrible person. Alone, I let the lies wash over me. Alone, I wrestled with sleep for hours through tears and unrelenting thoughts, until exhaustion finally took over and I fell asleep.

Numb, I walked through the next two days until the hearing. The judge decided to keep her in the custody of the state and assign her a guardian ad litem but would allow me to be her caretaker throughout the proceedings. I would get her back that evening from my mother-in-law's house. Hannah's father would post bail and stay with his mother throughout the trial. He would not be allowed to see her until he was charged or dismissed, which was fine with me. I was not certain I ever wanted to see him again. All I wanted was to get my baby girl back. So even though there were many state-ordered conditions to follow, I was overjoyed to have her back with me.

Reunited now with my precious girl, I rocked her in my arms and sang her to sleep as I had done every night since bringing her home, other than the last two nights when we were separated. She fell asleep with her little fist balled up next to her face as she frequently did. Before I laid her in her crib, I made her and myself a few promises. I did not know what we were going to do the next day about her care, as I had to go back to work and all my close relatives were working too. I did not know how I would pay the bills alone and be a single parent throughout the trial, but I promised her and myself that I would figure it out. I would be strong and never need anyone again. I would not cry anymore, and I would not fail again. I would be good enough and strong enough to care for her all on my own.

This may sound good, but I see now that in that moment, I took on a job that was not mine. I think I did this because of my husband's extreme betrayal. In that moment, I hardened my heart, faultily sealed up wounds that needed healing, and built armor that has never fit me. That night I became the tough, coldhearted, don't-need-no-one girl I thought I needed to be to move forward.

Up until the moment in the clearing outside my home office, sixteen years later, I had been that person. In every aspect of my life, I had projected that false self to everyone around me. I kept everyone and everything at arm's distance. Even before God, I performed as the strong independent girl who did not need anyone, even Him. After all, I feared trusting Him. I falsely blamed Him for what happened, even though I knew it was caused by the broken man who is now my ex-husband.

But that ill-fitting armor was heavy, and I was tired of carrying it around with me. I had never allowed the wounds to heal. Instead, they infected my whole being. God knew this and wanted me to be free. Free to be the real me—a tenderhearted little girl who needed a good Father. He saw through my facade, the overwhelming pain of betrayal, and the feelings of never being good enough, and He loved me too much to let me stay that way.

And here is the real kicker. He saw that I pretended to trust Him fully, knew that I really didn't, and loved me anyway.

But you, O Lord, are a God of compassion and mercy, slow to get angry and filled with unfailing love and faithfulness.
Psalm 86:15

What He wanted to show me, and all of us, is that we can come to Him with our self-made armor down and with our deepest pain exposed. Even though we don't trust Him fully, He will love us to restoration anyway. He knows we are made of dust and that we have an Enemy who continually works to separate us from Him. Our self-made armor is a scheme of the Enemy to keep us separated from God and our true selves, to keep us from being fully known and fully loved by God, and to keep us from walking in our original design, hand in hand with the Father. Satan works to keep us apart from full restoration by Jesus's sacrifice. When we are separated from God, we are not whole and truly ourselves; therefore, we are not the powerful force we are when we walk in our purpose.

I see now that the Enemy whispered those lies into my ears on those two lonely nights sixteen years earlier. After my ex-husband's betrayal, the devil convinced me that everyone in my life would do the same. Therefore I didn't heal of that wound. The Enemy also helped me create the ill-fitting armor of false strength and self-reliance. This armor kept me from God and my true self as I pretended to be something I was not, and it didn't allow me to heal from the pain that tore me apart.

But on that beautiful June morning, God revealed to me that I could now take off my armor. And I did. I stood fully exposed, fully known in the presence of God. My deepest pain and sin caused me to shake in my skin with shame, fearing that facing it would kill me. But I received only love—a love so ridiculously strong, it heals and restores even the deepest wound. A love that replaces weakness with strength. For He tells us "My grace is enough, it is all you need. My strength comes into its own in your weakness" (2 Corinthians 12:9 MSG). Amen.

Reflect: Instead of grieving with God and healing from my ex-husband's betrayal of my daughter and me, I made vows to be self-sufficient and strong.

I am protected

I didn't want to need anyone, even God, because I was afraid of being hurt again. But this self-made armor was terrible for me and grew increasingly tiresome to wear. It did not fit me, and it caused me to be something I was not. It kept me from healing.

What vows have you made to yourself in times of hardship?

_____

_____

_____

_____

Have these vows become ill-fitting armor?

_____

_____

_____

_____

El Shaddai

David tried to walk but he could hardly budge. David told Saul, "I can't even move with all this stuff on me. I'm not used to this." And he took it all off.
1 Samuel 17:38 MSG

Learning Love: The Armor David Didn't Wear

I have yet to meet a person who doesn't have a giant to face. Giants come in different forms for different people. Some of them will be present throughout our lives, but one thing remains true: God is with us.

You may know the story of David and Goliath, especially if you grew up going to Sunday school. However let's focus on the key to facing down the giants in our lives. When David stepped up to fight Goliath, the well-meaning Saul tried to give David standard soldier armor to protect him.

Read the story of David and Goliath from 1 Samuel.

> The things David was saying were picked up and reported to Saul. Saul sent for him.
>
> "Master," said David, "don't give up hope. I'm ready to go and fight this Philistine."
>
> Saul answered David, "You can't go and fight this Philistine. You're too young and inexperienced—and

he's been at this fighting business since before you were born."

David said, "I've been a shepherd, tending sheep for my father. Whenever a lion or bear came and took a lamb from the flock, I'd go after it, knock it down, and rescue the lamb. If it turned on me, I'd grab it by the throat, wring its neck, and kill it. Lion or bear, it made no difference—I killed it. And I'll do the same to this Philistine pig who is taunting the troops of God-Alive. God, who delivered me from the teeth of the lion and the claws of the bear, will deliver me from this Philistine."

Saul said, "Go. And God help you!"

Then Saul outfitted David as a soldier in armor. He put his bronze helmet on his head and belted his sword on him over the armor. David tried to walk but he could hardly budge.

David told Saul, "I can't even move with all this stuff on me. I'm not used to this." And he took it all off. (1 Samuel 17:31–39 MSG)

David put on the armor that worldly warriors would use to fight a giant. But Saul's armor did not fit David. So he took off the ill-fitting armor and won the battle with God as his offense and defense. David knew God's armor fit better than the soldier's armor, which fit so poorly it hindered his movement.

When we face giants, many things will look like the right type of armor for our hearts. However man-made armor is heavy and often hinders our movement and ability to overcome. David shows us that with God we do not need ill-fitting armor. Rather, we need faith that He will deliver us from the giants we face. He will show us how to take them down. He will protect us with His power.

Finding Freedom: Take Off the Ill-Fitting Armor

Release: Do you face any deep, open wounds (giants)?

_____

_____

_____

_____

What heavy, cumbersome pieces of armor do you wear? How do they hinder your healing?

_____

_____

_____

_____

Fly: Name the pieces of armor (vows, false identities, etc.) that you will take off now. Ask God to help you take them off and give them to Him.

Encouragement: God is the only armor we need for the battles we will face in our lifetime. "God is my shield, saving those whose hearts are true and right" (Psalm 7:10).

Let's Pray: *Father,* show us any ill-fitting armor that we may be carrying around and help us take it off. You are good and can be trusted to be our offense and defense. You are the one we can turn to for help in any battle we face. Thank you for being a good, good father. In Jesus Name, Amen.

Write your own prayer here:

_____

_____

_____

_____

_____

_____

_____

_____

_____

_____

_____

_____

_____

_____

_____

Chapter 6

PLAYGROUND MEMORY

The Lord doesn't see things the way you see them.
People judge by outward appearance,
but the Lord looks at the heart.
1 Samuel 16:7 NLT

I **THOUGHT I HAD GOTTEN** to the core of my false beliefs about God on that hard but healing morning outside my little office. But God wanted to go even deeper. He wanted to delve into my little-girl heart, wounded by the world and making me fell "less than." This belief led to poor choices in my teenage and young adult years, and that caused even more pain. Our actions are always indicators of our heart's beliefs (Proverbs 4:23).

One memory stands out from my third- or fourth-grade year. I know this memory is significant because it is one of the few clear memories I have from before age fifteen or so. Childhood was hard for me, and I think I purposely forgot most of it. I remember being teased a lot, but I honestly cannot remember what they said, except for this one vivid memory.

God brought this memory forward in my mind a few days into the journey, as I hiked into the forest down a well-known river trail near our town. I felt God saying, "Let's go back there. It's important to the story I am writing in you. It's important for this healing season."

I sat on a rock near the rushing creek and relived the memory, pouring it out on paper.

My friend and classmate David had also been relentlessly teased. As I look back with my adult eyes, I think he may have been homeless, or at least very poor. He wore the same pants and shirt every day, and all the other kids teased him because he did not smell good. I don't recall noticing that. He was kind and nice to me. That was all I required from a friend, probably because everyone else was always so cruel.

We played together every day at recess. Most of the time we walked to the far end of the playground, where the grass sloped down the hill a bit. We probably did this because nobody could see us. Our friendship was purely platonic, but we liked the reprieve from the usual playground torment. Sometimes we acted out a story I concocted. I was probably the leader of the event, since that was my personality.

I don't remember why, but one day, we decided to play on the yellow monkey bars. We sat talking on top of the bars. A couple of kids stood on the ground below singing, "Two little love birds sitting in a tree." Then they laughed and said, "Gross—the fat girl and the smelly kid. That's disgusting."

Tears rolled down my cheeks as I wrote this story. It was a defining moment for me. My soul cried out in anger at God as I sat on the rock by the creek.

God, where were you when this happened? It was so long ago, but it still hurts. I have never been the same since then. I've always thought something was wrong with me. That I was gross. That I was, as they said, the fat girl.

And like a warm blanket, God wrapped His arms around me. And this is what He said:

> Yes, this is where I wanted you to go. What I wanted you to see. Sweet, kind, tenderhearted girl, don't you see? You were kind to that little boy. You did not see his outsides like everyone else. You let him be himself, despite his one set of dirty clothes. And he was beautiful, wasn't he? I know; I made him too.
>
> You are beautiful as well. You're a sweet child, blind to people's outsides and drawn to their hearts. I made you that way. Will you be that way again? I know the world is cruel and it measures the outsides, even more so in the time of the world I have set you in. I know this is hard, but you have to deal with this brokenness. This is what I came to restore. It is awful to be judged and rejected based on your outsides. It breaks my heart too. Many people have been burned and scarred by this brokenness. I see them everywhere, and I know you do too.
>
> But you know the truth, and you always have.
>
> Beauty radiates from the inside out. I see the heart, and I judge from there.
>
> When I see you, I see a beautiful heart—a heart that needs healing from the pain of rejection. This is real pain, which I came to endure so I could restore people who would face it. You can let it go now. I came to restore you.
>
> The life abundant, the glorious life, comes when you refuse to conform to the world, which measures worth from the outside. That is a false standard, and it angers me. You feel my anger at the pain it has caused My precious children who are My works of art. How dare they call My art anything but perfect?
>
> I know you think you cannot let this one thing go. It has been with you so long, and it's your greatest fear.

Your deepest pain. The biggest lie you believe, my precious girl.

Can you believe Me about what I see? Can you believe Me when I say you are beautiful? That you are worthy? That you are good enough just as you are? Can you believe you don't have to try so hard to be what you think they want to see? You can be yourself. That is who I created you to be, and it is beautiful.

You should clothe yourselves with the beauty that comes from within, the unfading beauty of a gentle and quiet spirit, which is so precious to God
1 Peter 3:4

I sat there on the rock in tears. I wanted to believe the Lord, but I had many hurts, and I'd endured them for years. I needed to rebuild my foundation on these truths from God rather than the ones I'd learned from the world, but it would not be easy. These root lies embedded themselves so deeply in my heart, they had become my identity. I needed to rid myself of them.

God had taken me to the core of my heart and shown me His sadness for his little girl. He knew this was the place where I started believing I was less than His beautiful creation, and He wanted me to see His sadness as well. My healing began when I saw that my pain hurt Him as well. It felt like a friend sat there with me, acknowledging my pain as I grieved. God knows that grieving is part of healing. We often want to skip this part, but in order to tear down weak foundations and build strong ones in their place, we must face them.

Reflect: Cruel words other children spoke over me in my childhood became lies that I believed about myself. I carried them into my adulthood. They

I am a work of art

affected most of my decisions. God wanted me to see that I still believed lies spoken over me more than thirty years ago. And He wanted to heal them by bringing these memories back to my mind and showing me the truth.

Has someone spoken harsh words over you that made you feel "less than?"

_____

_____

_____

_____

_____

_____

Do you believe some part of you is not formed well?

_____

_____

_____

_____

_____

_____

The Way, the Truth, and the Life

Learning Love: David Anointed as King

Don't judge by his appearance or height, for I
have rejected him. The Lord doesn't see things the way you
see them. People judge by outward appearance,
but the Lord looks at the heart.
1 Samuel 16:7 NLT

The world's ways always oppose God's ways. This has been go-ing on forever. Humans, with our very limited sight, have always measured worth from the outside. God has always measured the heart.

Our brokenness causes people to judge others by their outsides. Even Adam and Eve immediately experienced shame about their bodies after eating from the forbidden tree. It is a fact that we must endure as we walk through this broken world.

Even people of God, such as Samuel, judge people by their outside appearances.

> "Yes," Samuel replied. "I have come to sacrifice to the Lord. Purify yourselves and come with me to the sacri-fice." Then Samuel performed the purification rite for Jesse and his sons and invited them to the sacrifice, too.
> When they arrived, Samuel took one look at Eliab and thought, "Surely this is the Lord's anointed!"
> But the Lord said to Samuel, "Don't judge by his

appearance or height, for I have rejected him. The Lord doesn't see things the way you see them. People judge by outward appearance, but the Lord looks at the heart." (1 Samuel 16:5–7)

God had to remind Samuel, His faithful prophet, not to look at Jesse's sons' outsides to pick the new king. Samuel was impressed with the tall and strapping men he saw before him, but God rebuked him.

God knew that none of these men, despite their fine outward appearances, had a servant's heart like David. But David wasn't in the lineup, because his father didn't think he was king material.

We see here, and again and again throughout the Bible, that all humans judge people on appearance. But God, the only rightful judge, judges the heart.

Therefore we must go to God for our validation and not allow the world to define us. This doesn't mean the world won't judge us and find us lacking. It means we will learn to recognize when we have been judged, and we will bring it to God for His rightful judgement.

When we do this, we learn about grace. When God declared David fit to rule His nation, He knew David would sleep with Bathsheba, impregnate her, and kill her husband to try and cover his sin. And yet God still called him.

God sees us through the eyes of His mercy and grace. He sees us through Jesus's blood, which covers our sins and makes us righteous in Him. He knows we are frail and broken, but He still wants to work with us in our mess. He is simply looking for our willingness. David was willing to humble himself and be led by God.

This must be your truth. Our kind, loving God already sees you through the blood of Jesus. Go to God for His judgement of who you are. You are His dearly loved child, and He wants nothing more than to love you. Let Him.

Finding Freedom: Determine Your Assessor

Release: Do you have painful memories of being judged?

_____

_____

_____

_____

_____

Do you think God allows you to remember these incidents or even brings them back to you because they are significant to your perception of yourself?

_____

_____

_____

_____

_____

Have you ever let God give you His perspective on the memory? Have you allowed God to be the only judge?

_____

_____

_____

_____

_____

_____

_____

_____

Fly: Spend time with God around a memory in which someone judged you and said untrue things about you. Talk with God about how their judgements changed your perception of yourself. Allow God to open this wound and then show you His perspective. Allow Him to be the One to judge you.

Encouragement: At the feast, Jesus said, "Look beneath the surface so you can judge correctly" (John 7:24). The Bible mentions the topic of judging several times because it is a common issue.

Let's Pray: _Father_, we know You are the only rightful judge, and you judge by the heart rather than outward appearances. Our world judges others, however, and tells lies that hurt us. Help us to see truth and hear what You say about us. In Jesus's name, amen.

Write your own prayer here:

REBUILDING ON THE TRUTH

A final word: Be strong in the Lord and in his mighty
power. Put on all of God's armor so that you will be able
to stand firm against all strategies of the devil.
For we are not fighting against flesh-and-blood enemies,
but against evil rulers and authorities of the unseen
world, against mighty powers in this dark world,
and against evil spirits in the heavenly places.
Therefore, put on every piece of God's armor so you will be
able to resist the enemy in the time of evil.
Then after the battle you will still be standing firm.
Ephesians 6:10–13 NLT

WITH MY HEART OPEN AND displaying the deep-seated lies I have carried so long, I could see my identity needed to change. I needed
to rebuild my identity on God's truths rather than on the lies I had
allowed to identify me. But how?

Saying that our identities are found in Christ sounds nice, but it's not natural in a world that constantly tries to identify us. But God, in His amazing compassion toward me, did not leave me to figure out how to recreate my identity on my own. He came alongside me through devotionals, sermons, friends, and the Holy Spirit's insight as I opened my Bible and searched for answers. And then He revealed something amazing: an instruction manual in the book of Ephesians, teaching me how to recreate my identity by using spiritual armor.

Through studying Ephesians I learned that God's plan is, and has been through all generations, to restore us to His original design, loved as His children and free to be all He created us to be. Paul, the author of Ephesians, concludes the book by inciting us to put on the armor of God (Ephesians 6:10–20).

The armor of God reveals truth and shows us how to rebuild our new identities as loved and free in Christ. And once our new identities are built, our armor keeps us safe and keeps our integrity intact during daily battles. It starts with the belt of truth, which reveals the foundational truth about who God says we are—the only measurement that matters. Next, the breastplate of righteousness shows us how to surrender control and find the real life our hearts were designed for. The shoes of peace help us walk in the new life God redeemed us for.

God also gives us the shield of faith, which helps us define our gifts and calling, and the helmet of salvation reminds us to stay in step with God in order to stay on course. And finally, we use the sword of the Spirit to defend ourselves against the Enemy's attacks against our new identities in Christ. The armor of God is both the process of rebuilding and the daily armor we need to continue in our God-given identities.

We know God constantly works on us until the day we come home. He is in the business of restoration. He pulls down strongholds by working deeply and gently within us. He restores, redeems, and brings the freedom needed for glorious living with Him.

In this section, we will walk through the process God used to rebuild my identity on truth. It covers the first three pieces of armor and includes stories and practical application activities to get these truths deep in our hearts. Knowing the truth and believing the truth are not the same. It takes time and dedication to tear down lies and rebuild with truth. Plus, we have to continue to live in a broken world and engage in spiritual battle for the rest of our time on earth.

As we wrestle with our hearts through these applications, we move closer to our created selves, but we must remember this is not just a list to check off. Perfection in walking with God is neither required nor possible. We will fail, and so will our family and friends, but His mercy is new every day for all of us. We must discern what is from God and what is from the broken world, the Enemy, or our broken selves. And we aren't going to get that right all the time. Sometimes, especially at first, we may get it wrong more often than we get it right. It's a lot like being a child. Remember, we are born into new lives now. We'll need to learn to live in our new lives like newborn babies, which may take a while.

So give yourself a big break, and let's start building on God's truth.

WHO GOD SAYS WE ARE

*It's in Christ that we find out who we are
and what we are living for.*
Ephesians 1:11 MSG

ON VACATION A COUPLE YEARS ago, our family took the river path from town back to our camp. By God's grace, my family now consisted of my new husband, Matthew; our two little boys; and Hannah, whom Matthew had adopted. My youngest son, age four at the time, rode his strider bike while I walked beside him. We met another family coming from the opposite direction and needed to move over to make room for them on the narrow path. Oddly, the smallest boy in that family made a face at my little one and yelled, "Stupid baby!"

Shocked, I hesitated. Did we know this family? I didn't recognize them. As I tried to figure out what had just happened, I barely noticed my brokenhearted child, who'd dropped his bike and slunk into the bushes on the side of the path, an expression of worthlessness spackled all over his sweet face.

I knew how he was feeling, having been belittled since my early childhood. My furiously protective mama side kicked in. In an instant, I plucked him out of the bush, laid my cheek on his, and whispered truth into his ear and straight to his broken heart.

I asked him if he knew that little boy, though I already had the answer. He shook his head, unable to speak through the hot tears I could feel rolling onto my own cheeks.

"Precious boy, that boy does not know you," I said. "But Mama knows you, and Mama thinks you are smart and kind. Mama thinks you are sweet and fun and funny. Mama knows you and loves every part of you, my precious boy." And with tears rolling down both our faces now, I held him until I could feel he'd let my words roll over the other boy's words.

Has a person or a circumstance in life made you believe you are anything less than the precious child of God that you are? Do you need to crawl up in God's lap and let Him speak these words over your heart?

God wants to tell you that you are His precious child and that He created you uniquely and wonderfully. He calls you His work of art, and He is delighted with you—the real you. He wants to whisper these words to your soul until they roll over everything the broken world

So you have not recieved a spirit that makes you fearful slaves. Instead, you received God's Spirit when he adopted you as his own children. Now we call him, "Abba, Father." For his Spirit joins with our spirit to affirm that we are God's children.
Romans 8:15-16

and the destructive Enemy have told you about yourself. He wants to hold you cheek to cheek until you believe you are wonderfully made, a work of art formed by the master craftsman, and tell you that He is delighted with you.

I know you don't fully believe that yet. I did not believe it either, and some days I still don't. But I've grown a lot and most days I do believe that He delights in me, and you will get there too. Along the way, I will be praying for you.

Reflect: A child whom my son did not even know labeled and shamed him. This isn't the last time someone will speak lies over my child, so it was important to me to speak the

I am a child of God

truth over him. God wants to do the same for us. He wants us all to know we are His children. Our identities come from being His children. Period. Being His children is the only thing that gives us significance, value, and worth.

You are God's precious child. He created you uniquely and wonderfully. He is delighted with you. How do you feel when you read these statements? (Be honest with yourself. It is okay to struggle to believe.) Have you ever thought of your identity as a child of God? How does that change how you see yourself?

_____

_____

_____

_____

_____

_____

_____

_____

_____

Abba

Learning Love: Chosen Children

Read Paul's encouraging words in Ephesians chapter 1.

> All praise to God, the Father of our Lord Jesus Christ, who has blessed us with every spiritual blessing in the heavenly realms because we are united with Christ.
>
> Even before he made the world, God loved us and chose us in Christ to be holy and without fault in his eyes.
>
> God decided in advance to adopt us into his own family by bringing us to himself through Jesus Christ. This is what he wanted to do, and it gave him great pleasure. So we praise God for the glorious grace he has poured out on us who belong to his dear Son. He is so rich in kindness and grace that he purchased our freedom with the blood of his Son and forgave our sins. He has showered his kindness on us, along with all wisdom and understanding.
>
> God has now revealed to us his mysterious will regarding Christ—which is to fulfill his own good plan. And this is the plan: At the right time he will bring everything together under the authority of Christ—everything in heaven and on earth. Furthermore, because we are united with Christ, we have received an inheritance

from God, for he chose us in advance, and he makes everything work out according to his plan.

God's purpose was that we Jews who were the first to trust in Christ would bring praise and glory to God.

And now you Gentiles have also heard the truth, the Good News that God saves you. And when you believed in Christ, he identified you as his own by giving you the Holy Spirit, whom he promised long ago.

The Spirit is God's guarantee that he will give us the inheritance he promised and that He has purchases us to be his own people. He did this so we would praise and glorify him.

Ever since I first heard of your strong faith in the Lord Jesus and your love for God's people everywhere, I have not stopped thanking God for you. I pray for you constantly, asking God, the glorious Father of our Lord Jesus Christ, to give you spiritual wisdom and insight so that you might grow in your knowledge of God. I pray that your hearts will be flooded with light so that you can understand the confident hope he has given to those he called—his holy people who are his rich and glorious inheritance.

I also pray that you will understand the incredible greatness of God's power for us who believe him. This is the same mighty power that raised Christ from the dead and seated him in the place of honor at God's right hand in the heavenly realms. Now he is far above any ruler or authority or power or leader or anything else— not only in this world but also in the world to come. God has put all things under the authority of Christ and has made him head over all things for the benefit of the church. And the church is his body; it is made full and complete by Christ, who fills all things everywhere with himself. (Ephesians 1:3–23 NLT)

In Ephesians chapter one, God reveals the foundational truth that we are His chosen children. His plan all along has been to adopt us through Christ and to redeem us and restore us to our original design. His design. His work of art. Nothing could increase our value more than knowing we were created by the Maker of the universe and then redeemed through the blood of Christ. This truth can and should be the only basis for our value.

However this is not the case with most of us. We often let the world determine our worthiness. Our value comes from the approval of others instead of God. We call ourselves worthy when we accomplish what the world has deemed successful. But our worth should come from the fact that Jesus redeemed us. To find our true, freeing identities, we must change the way we think.

When we change our foundational beliefs about our significance, God will restore us to our rightful identities. This restoration comes when we learn the truth and live it, letting it sink into both our heads and hearts. Truth and trust go together. We must believe that what God says about us is truth. That His Word in Ephesians is the truth. That His plan is good. That He loves and that He is and always has been in control. He has unfolded the plan and wants to restore us to His design.

In light of God's truth revealed in Ephesians chapter one, reject any root lies that were revealed to you as you read the last sections. Let His words speak truth into your life as you begin to believe them. I know believing is hard. I am not saying this is going to be a magic, overnight, one-prayer-and-it's-gone restoration. Rather, you will need to meditate on the truth, fight the darts the Enemy throws at you, and capture every thought that does not line up with this truth.

This is the armor of God. It starts with the belt of truth. All the other pieces of armor connect to this truth.

This will be an epic battle for freedom. And it will be worth it.

Finding Freedom: Loved and Free Manifesto—the Belt of Truth

Release: How does the truth about being a child of God, adopted through the blood of Christ, resonate with you? Do you struggle to believe the truth?

_____

_____

_____

_____

_____

Jesus loved you enough to die for you. How does that fact change the measure you use to value yourself?

_____

_____

_____

_____

_____

Fly: God helped me to create a Loved and Free Manifesto to help the truth sink in: that I am a dearly loved child of God, valuable enough to die for. It personalizes the truths found in Ephesians chapter one. I couldn't believe them until I had read my manifesto every day for a long time. I still read it often. Write out this manifesto and put it somewhere you will see often. This is the belt of truth that holds up the rest of your armor.

Loved and Free Manifesto

Genesis 1:26: I am a dearly loved child of God, created in His image with a special purpose to reflect and glorify Him.

Ephesians 1:4: Long before God made the world, He loved me and chose me to be the focus of His love. I am loved unconditionally.

Ephesians 1:5: I am adopted into God's family through the blood of Christ. I was chosen. I belong.

Ephesians 1:6: I am loved enough to die for, regardless of what I have or have not done. This is my approval, the only affirmation I need. I am good enough as I am.

Ephesians 1:7: Jesus saved and covered me, which frees me to be me. I am abundantly free.

- I am free from striving to prove my worth.
- I am free from others' opinions of me.
- I am free from comparing myself to others.
- I am free to be who God created me to be.

Ephesians 1:9–10: In His love I find the glorious life He planned for me. He placed desires in my heart during my creation.

Ephesians 1:13: I am filled with the Holy Spirit, and with Him I find the love that fills me and frees my heart to be who He created me to be.

Ephesians 1:18: God desires His best for me and always works things out for my good. He has a glorious life planned for me.

Ephesians 1:19–20: God is in complete control, there is no authority above Him, and I am an important part of His plan.

Ephesians 1:23: God loves me dearly and is always with me and for me.

Encouragement: Every day is a battle for your soul. Every day the Enemy tries to take you out with lies. Every day you walk through a broken world filled with brokenness and wrong beliefs. Every day you need God's strength, which comes from knowing the truth. The truth sets us free. "And you will know the truth, and the truth will set you free" (John 8:32) NLT.

Let's Pray: *Papa*, You are a good, good Father who desires healing and restoration for His children. You are near to the brokenhearted and make whole those who seek You. In You we find out who we are. Reveal to us Your truth today as we seek You. Amen.

Write your own prayer here:

_____

_____

_____

_____

_____

_____

_____

_____

Chapter 8

SACRIFICING THE STRONGHOLD

For we are God's masterpiece. He created us anew in
Christ Jesus, so we can do the good things he planned
for us long ago.
Ephesians 2:10 NLT

A FEW WEEKS AFTER I started my daily habit of repeating the truth of who God said I was, my perspective on my current role at work changed. I no longer sought the promotion. I realized I had been fixated on gaining the promotion and an important title only because I thought it would give me the stamp of approval my low self-worth needed. The title would prove I was good enough, or so I thought.

I started to understand that I did not even desire to be a senior sales leader. I was woefully burned out of fixing the same work issues for the past fifteen years. For the first time, I saw that I longed to do something else entirely.

But what? I was afraid to make a change. This had been my role for years. It was still our main source of income, and it provided healthcare coverage for my family of five. I could not just pick up and leave, even if my heart whispered longings for other things.

But I could not let go of the feeling that I wanted change. I polished up my résumé and applied at a few new places to no avail. Still the thoughts persisted.

A few weeks later, obedience to God and the need for a career change weighed heavily on my heart. I packed up my mountain bike and rode far into the forest as I often do when I need to talk with God.

Throughout the push to the top of the trail, I wrestled with God about what I thought I could hear Him telling me to do. I had known for about a month that God had asked me to quit my job. But I had been trying to rationalize with Him and tell Him it didn't make sense. And it didn't, if I used my natural eyes. After all, just a few months ago, He had told me to stay in that role. My human logic wrestled with the sudden change, but my heart knew the truth.

By the time I reached the top of the trail, my heart had begun to surrender. I had given God all the excuses I could muster up. The answer was not changing. So I sat on a fallen log, took out my phone notepad, and poured out this prayer:

> *Father*, I know what I must do. I hear Your still, small voice through the shouts of fear and distraction. Just barely.
>
> It makes sense in a spiritual way that You would ask me to sacrifice the deepest idol of my heart—the remaining stronghold keeping me from You and from all You've created me to be. We've been here before, You and me. You are always with me.
>
> You are the provider. I'm not. You always have been. I never have been. You took care of me even when I thought I was self-sufficient. You led me even when I

did not know I was following. Silly me. Thank You for taking care of me. I know You will again.

You are faithful, Papa. I will take Your hand and step even deeper into the unknown because You have called me here. Above all else, I want more of You. This is the deepest desire of my heart. You will wait for me here until I follow, but I distance myself from You when I'm afraid to go with You. I want to be with You. I want to be what You say I can be.

This is the point where I pivot. I denounce the lie that I was abandoned to take care of myself and that I am not good enough to be what You've called me to be. The lie that I have to pretend to be someone I am not. This is the point where I tell the Enemy I no longer believe those lies, and I take my Father's hand as He leads me to the next place He has for me.

This is scary and it looks like a stupid move, but faith is the hope of things not seen, and with my spiritual eyes, it makes all kinds of sense. It is tangibly the release of my self-reliance and working for approval, of the strongholds that bind my heart and keep me from the best God has for me. To follow through, I must believe God is the provider, and I am not. I must believe God says I am good enough, that He created me purposefully and has better for me than pretending to be someone I am not.

I must believe that when I get to the mountain (otherwise known as Monday) to sacrifice that which binds my heart and separates me from a deeper relationship with God, I will see an open window.

I have to surrender to His good plan for me.

"For I know the plans I have for you," says the Lord. *"They are plans for good and not for disaster, to give you a future and a hope."*
Jer 29:11

I am set free

Reflect: God asked me to be radical and release one of the strongholds in my heart. A stronghold is a strongly defended belief. I truly believed I had to be the provider and therefore was not free to be who I wanted to be. So God asked me to quit my job, which was not rational at the time, and to trust Him to provide. Interstingly, I see in hindsight that God did not ask me to do this until I was ready. In fact, He asked me to stay in the demoted position for several months while I healed from the pain of demotion and broke free from my wrong identity. All along, God planned to bring down this stronghold in my heart and, as I surrendered, to set me free.

Do you have any strongholds in your life that may require a sacrifice? To identify them, think about the things that have continued coming up throughout your healing journey.

_____

_____

_____

_____

Do these beliefs line up with what you have learned about God's character so far?

_____

_____

_____

_____

Learning Love: The Lord Will Provide

Read the story of Abraham and Isaac from Genesis chapter 22.

> Some time later, God tested Abraham's faith. "Abraham!" God called.
>
> "Yes," he replied. "Here I am."
>
> "Take your son, your only son—yes, Isaac, whom you love so much—and go to the land of Moriah. Go and sacrifice him as a burnt offering on one of the mountains, which I will show you."
>
> The next morning Abraham got up early. He saddled his donkey and took two of his servants with him, along with his son, Isaac. Then he chopped wood for a fire for a burnt offering and set out for the place God had told him about.
>
> On the third day of their journey, Abraham looked up and saw the place in the distance.
>
> "Stay here with the donkey," Abraham told the servants. "The boy and I will travel a little farther. We will worship there, and then we will come right back."
>
> So Abraham placed the wood for the burnt offering on Isaac's shoulders, while he himself carried the fire and the knife. As the two of them walked on together,
>
> Isaac turned to Abraham and said, "Father?"
>
> "Yes, my son?" Abraham replied.

"We have the fire and the wood," the boy said, "but where is the sheep for the burnt offering?"

"God will provide a sheep for the burnt offering, my son," Abraham answered. And they both walked on together.

When they arrived at the place where God had told him to go, Abraham built an altar and arranged the wood on it. Then he tied his son, Isaac, and laid him on the altar on top of the wood. And Abraham picked up the knife to kill his son as a sacrifice.

At that moment the angel of the Lord called to him from heaven, "Abraham! Abraham!"

"Yes," Abraham replied. "Here I am!"

"Don't lay a hand on the boy!" the angel said. "Do not hurt him in any way, for now I know that you truly fear God. You have not withheld from me even your son, your only son."

Then Abraham looked up and saw a ram caught by its horns in a thicket. So he took the ram and sacrificed it as a burnt offering in place of his son.

Abraham named the place Yahweh-Yireh (which means "the Lord will provide"). To this day, people still use that name as a proverb: "On the mountain of the Lord it will be provided."

Then the angel of the Lord called again to Abraham from heaven.

"This is what the Lord says: Because you have obeyed me and have not withheld even your son, your only son, I swear by my own name that I will certainly bless you. I will multiply your descendants beyond number, like the stars in the sky and the sand on the seashore. Your descendants will conquer the cities of their enemies." (Genesis 22:1–17)

This story is hard for us to read. We wonder how Abraham was okay with this command from God. How could the good God ask a father to kill his own son? There are lots of signs throughout the story, however, that point out that Abraham had faith that God would provide a lamb or somehow perform a miracle that would save Isaac's life. Abraham's told his servants that he and Isaac would return. This is the key to this act of obedience. Abraham had been tested before and knew who his God was. He knew his God was good, and therefore, he knew his God would do something radical and good with his radical obedience.

It certainly was not easy for Abraham to obey. We often wait to obey because we first want to understand how God will come through for us. But that is not how God works. He uses tough things to build our faith by keeping us in the dark while He works out the details. In fact, faith means the hope for that which is unseen. It would not be faith if we knew the outcome. Instead, God bolsters our faith and provides the way—two good things out of one radical act of obedience.

Now read Genesis 22:15–17 again.

> Then the angel of the Lord called again to Abraham from heaven. "This is what the Lord says: Because you have obeyed me and have not withheld even your son, your only son, I swear by my own name that I will certainly bless you. I will multiply your descendants beyond number, like the stars in the sky and the sand on the seashore. Your descendants will conquer the cities of their enemies. (Genesis 22:15–17)

This is the outcome of Abraham's obedience. God blesses him with more than He promised him because Abraham had faith that God would keep His promise and provide a way for him.

Finding Freedom: Surrender to Freedom—The Breastplate of Righteousness

Release: Have you identified any strongholds in your life that may require a sacrifice?

Ask God if you need to destroy anything before you can move to the next place He has for you.

_____

_____

_____

_____

Fly: God will ask you to surrender and obey because He wants to give you a better life. He wants to give you the dreams of your heart. He will ask you to destroy your idols. He is not afraid to ask us to do something that scares us half to death in order to reveal that we trust something else more than we trust Him. Then He can give us the better He has for us.

Surrendering to God's design brings us closer to the right relationship and peace we found in the garden. It sets us free! And I don't know about you, but life in the garden of Eden sounds nice right now, compared to the brutal tyranny of following my fleshly desire and trying to control my life.

Putting on the Breastplate of Righteousness Activity

Read Paul's words from Ephesians chapter 2.

> It wasn't so long ago that you were mired in that old stagnant life of sin. You let the world, which doesn't know the first thing about living, tell you how to live. You filled your lungs with polluted unbelief, and then exhaled disobedience. We all did it, all of us doing what we felt like doing, when we felt like doing it, all of us in the same boat. It's a wonder God didn't lose his temper and do away with the whole lot of us. Instead, immense in mercy and with an incredible love, he embraced us. He took our sin-dead lives and made us alive in Christ. He did all this on his own, with no help from us! Then he picked us up and set us down in highest heaven in company with Jesus, our Messiah.
>
> Now God has us where he wants us, with all the time in this world and the next to shower grace and kindness upon us in Christ Jesus. Saving is all his idea, and all his work. All we do is trust him enough to let him do it. It's God's gift from start to finish! We don't play the major role. If we did, we'd probably go around bragging that we'd done the whole thing! No, we neither make nor save ourselves. God does both the making and saving. He creates each of us by Christ Jesus to join him in the work he does, the good work he has gotten ready for us to do, work we had better be doing. (Ephesians 2:1–10 MSG)

God came to save us and put us back into a right relationship with Him so we could follow Him instead of the ways of the world (Ephesians 2:2). This is our righteousness, a pure gift (Ephesians 2:8), regardless of how our life has gone thus far. Surrendering to God's saving grace and His plan for our lives is how we put on the breastplate of righteousness. We know we can do nothing to earn righteousness, so instead we surrender to what He has done for us (Ephesians 2:9).

In surrendering our will, we find restoration to the life our hearts were designed for. We find freedom because we are fully known and fully loved by the Creator and Author of life and because He wants us to do the good things He predestined for us (Ephesians 2:10). We think it will be hard to give up and let someone else have control. But when we do, the chains break and souls go free. When we surrender to God, we find the freedom we've always searched for.

God works on our hearts and in our lives in seasons. He is always on the move, restoring us to His original design, until the day we go home. We would be overwhelmed if He restored us all at once. So God works in seasons. And just like the natural seasons—death and waiting, resurrection and new sprouting, growth and flourishing, and harvest time—we find different purposes in different times. The key to finding freedom, in whatever season God has us in, is to let God author the season and then surrender to it.

As a judicious planner, otherwise known as a control freak, surrendering was hard for me. But I found it so freeing that I never want to live any other way again. God showed me how to live and surrender to His seasonal ways, allowing Him to author the season. Even better, I learned to define what success looked like in that season by using the prayer template below. Pray and seek God with these questions. His answers will become your focus for this season.

Surrendering to God's Season Questionnaire

- Lord, what do I need to surrender in this season in order to be closer to You?
- Lord, what is keeping me from being all you have created me to be, and what are You restoring this season?

- Do I walk in any wrong ways or beliefs that You would like me to put to death?
- Lord, tell me about the season You have me in. Give me some words or a message to live by right now.
- What would you like me to learn about You or myself during this timeframe?
- What are the most important things in this season (goals, accomplishments, new truths)?
- What does success look like for me in this season? What do You want me to accomplish for Your kingdom during this time?
- What Scripture speaks to the season I'm in and that I can remind myself of when I struggle with doubts?

Encouragement: God speaks to us and we can recognize His voice. We need to seek and believe. Discern using the Bible and obey what He says. "My sheep recognize my voice. I know them, and they follow me" (John 10:27 MSG).

Let's Pray: *Lord,* we long to obey You and follow You and Your good plan. We know we are set free in surrender. It is hard sometimes, though. Give us the faith we need to believe and the strength we need to obey. Help us recognize Your voice so we can follow You. In Jesus's name, amen.

Write your own prayer here:

_____

_____

_____

_____

RELENTLESSLY PURSUANT LOVE

*May you experience the love of Christ, though it is too
great to understand fully. Then you will be made complete with all the fullness of life and power that comes
from God. Now all glory to God, who is able, through his
mighty power at work within us, to accomplish infinitely
more than we might ask or think.*

Ephesians 3:19–20

I QUIT MY JOB THAT Monday as God asked of me. I had not heard
from God on how it would work out. I just knew it was what He
was calling me to do, so I obeyed. Even though our life was still
in turmoil with our daughter at the therapy camp and her medical
bills looming, I obeyed. It was terrifying and so scary, in fact, that
I had a panic attack a few days later.

Upon my resignation on Monday, my boss had asked me to
hold tight until the next day and talk to the senior vice president
about my decision. My resignation had taken him aback. Over and
over, he told me it was a bad move because of the pending changes
coming from the recent acquisition. On Tuesday, I became ill with

a stomach bug and could not make it in to work. I think they thought I was hiding from them, but I truly was violently ill, both physically and mentally.

As I lay in bed, sick with the muscle aches and nausea that come with a stomach bug, my relentless doubts plagued me. All the questions my boss had asked me and the doubts he'd introduced had me questioning God's plan. I thought I would get instant revelation from God when I took the leap of faith to quit. Instead, I got sick and struggled with doubts about the next step. God seemed suddenly to go radio silent, and I started imagining all kinds of doomsday scenarios. Had I misheard God and done something insane? Would they walk me out today with no chance or time to look for a different position internally, now that I had finally stood up to them? Would they refuse to give me a reference for the eleven good years I had put in? Would we lose our home in Durango and have to move to a city we despised so I could get a new corporate job I didn't want? I had to ensure we could take care of our family financially.

But my biggest fear was that I had messed up our lives and misheard God. While I had been sure of God's command just a few days prior, doubt had taken over again, choking my faith in God and making me grasp for control. I was back to believing I had to figure all this out now that it hadn't gone as I'd planned. I had to stay in control. Me, myself, and I.

Overwhelmed and unsure of what to do, I had a panic attack. I could not rest, despite the need to overcome the stomach bug. My doubts would not stop their vicious parade through my mind. My chest was tight, and I labored to breathe. My heart raced, and my limbs shook. I knew this was more than the physical illness caused by the rotavirus. I thought I alone had to fix what I'd broken. The weight of that belief crushed my soul and nearly killed my physical body.

I was not strong enough to carry this weight on my own. I was not made to.

If God loved me so much and He was so good, I thought, then why had my life been so hard? Why did He keep making me go through all this? What good was coming from it? How could He be good when all I saw was bad?

But I also knew that even though I blamed God for many of these things, He still came after me to save me. I knew He was not to blame for all the brokenness. I had falsely accused Him for years when He wanted to redeem these broken parts of my story.

So even though I made the first move toward quitting, fear grabbed me. I panicked and quickly reverted to my old beliefs. But God was not moved. I was just like Peter, who stepped out of the boat onto the water, took a few steps, got scared, and started sinking. Then Jesus grabbed him.

Jesus grabbed me too and said the same thing to me He said to Peter. "Why did you doubt?" (Matthew 14:31 NIV).

A month before, I would have thought that was a condemning question, rebuking me for my lack of faith and proving once again that I was not good enough. I would have thought God was showing me I did not measure up to the faith He required of someone who was called to do amazing things with Him. But now I knew God never corrects in shame, so I knew He hadn't meant it that way.

He knows what we are made of and that we live in a broken world with a scheming Enemy. The odds stack against us, and we could never make it alone. That is why He sent His Son to set us free from the brokenness and to give us a glorious new life found in Him. This is not because of anything we do but because of who He is. He is love. Not fear, not shame. Love. And His love has the power to redeem all things, rewriting stories in the process.

He wants to rewrite all our stories as fully loved and fully free so we can step into the better story He has already planned for us. This is the gospel. The most epic story of love ever written.

God rewrote the story of the broken world, with a love so extravagant it would endure the worst kind of pain and death, to win back even the hearts of those who blamed Him. He loves us so extravagantly that He rewrote the story on a grand scale for each person who opens the door to Him and invites Him in. Each and every one. Including me.

Yes, you came when I called; you told me, "do not fear."
Lord, you have come to my defense; you have redeemed my life.
Lam 3:57-58

And isn't this the kind of love my heart longs for? A never-failing love, a love that chases me down and thinks I'm beautiful and worthy, even in my worst days of doubt. His love heals and restores my broken heart from the pain my brokenness has caused me, bolsters my faith, and keeps me moving forward.

I want my story to be one of unfailing love. I think we all do.

Looking back a few months, I see that God had a plan for me that I could never have imagined. For several weeks I endured my superiors' request for me to stay and help with my transition, but with no clear answers on how long this would last. My fear in the waiting made me lean hard on God with the little faith I could muster. But after a few weeks, God came through in a radical way. He provided a new opportunity at my same company on the product team, a position that hadn't existed there just a month earlier. It was the same position I had applied to at other companies when I was first demoted and a role I had been longing for.

Can you believe that?

God is so good! He knew what I wanted and needed: healing. If I had moved into this new position sooner, I would have made the same mistake as before: turning my job into my identity. So He made me walk through the doubt, weed the lies out of my heart, and increase my faith, all while He built a new way for me.

God is so good. He can build our characters and give us the desires of our hearts by taking us down paths we never have chosen for ourselves. He can pull rotten things from our hearts through the hard parts of our stories and then surprise us with something much better in the same chapter. Our stories have highs, lows, and many mundane moments between. But God uses every part for our good as we trust in Him.

He is the redeemer of our past and author of our future. And He is writing an epic love story in every moment of your life right now.

Reflect: Just like Peter, I had strong faith as I stepped out of the boat (talked to my boss about resigning), but as soon as I saw the waves and the water (my boss asked questions

I am redeemed

I was not prepared for), I started sinking in my own doubt. Most of my doubt came from a wrong view of the story of my life and God's hand in it. I had not seen the amazing redemption He had given in the hard times of my life, so my faith wavered when the waves came up.

Do you see God's redemptive power in the hardships you have gone through?

_____

_____

_____

_____

_____

How strong is your faith when the storms of life come up?

_____

_____

_____

_____

El Sali

Learning Love: The Power of Redemptive Love

Read in Luke about the shame Peter felt when he denied Christ.

> So they arrested him and led him to the high priest's home. And Peter followed at a distance. The guards lit a fire in the middle of the courtyard and sat around it, and Peter joined them there. A servant girl noticed him in the firelight and began staring at him. Finally she said, "This man was one of Jesus's followers!"
>
> But Peter denied it. "Woman," he said, "I don't even know him!" After a while someone else looked at him and said, "You must be one of them!"
>
> "No, man, I'm not!" Peter retorted.
>
> About an hour later someone else insisted, "This must be one of them, because he is a Galilean, too."

But Peter said, "Man, I don't know what you are talking about." And immediately, while he was still speaking, the rooster crowed.

At that moment the Lord turned and looked at Peter. Suddenly, the Lord's words flashed through Peter's mind: "Before the rooster crows tomorrow morning, you will deny three times that you even know me." And Peter left the courtyard, weeping bitterly. (Luke 22:54–64 NLT)

Now read this interaction between Peter and Jesus from John.

After breakfast Jesus asked Simon Peter, "Simon son of John, do you love me more than these?"

"Yes, Lord," Peter replied, "you know I love you."

"Then feed my lambs," Jesus told him.

Jesus repeated the question: "Simon son of John, do you love me?"

"Yes, Lord," Peter said, "you know I love you."

"Then take care of my sheep," Jesus said.

A third time he asked him, "Simon son of John, do you love me?"

Peter was hurt that Jesus asked the question a third time. He said, "Lord, you know everything. You know that I love you."

Jesus said, "Then feed my sheep"

"I tell you the truth, when you were young, you were able to do as you liked; you dressed yourself and went wherever you wanted to go. But when you are old, you will stretch out your hands, and others will dress you and take you where you don't want to go." Jesus said this to let him know by what kind of death he would glorify God. Then Jesus told him, "Follow me." (John 21:15–19 NLT)

After Peter denies Jesus, He does something amazing, which shows us how God forgives and renews us when our doubt causes us to sin.

First, we see Peter's humanity and how his denial caused him shame. We know from the text that Peter "wept bitterly" after the rooster crowed. Peter lived in his shame until Jesus touched him.

When I am living in shame, negative thoughts overwhelm me. I think I'm not good enough or faithful enough. During a big mess up, those thoughts parade through my mind until I start to believe them. Peter, a human like me who had the same Enemy I have today, would have experienced similar shame.

Three times Jesus asks Peter if he loves Him. Then Jesus forgives and reaffirms him despite his failures. Furthermore, Jesus invites Peter to "follow Him" and "feed His sheep," despite his failing. Peter's story is rewritten in this moment. God redeems his failures with His love for Peter, then He sets him back on the path of discipleship. Peter later becomes one of the founders of the Christian church.

This story is such a great example of how God redeems and rewrites our stories again and again—as many times as we veer off the path and need His help to get back on the right path. If we turn back to God and allow Him, He forgives us with His unfailing love. Then He redeems our failures, as Jesus did with Peter, allowing us to learn and be strengthened from them. Finally, He sets us back on the right path to follow Him into the glorious life He has predestined for us.

Finding Freedom: The Redeemed Story—The Shoes of Peace

Release: Have you ever thought about God's grand story—the fall of man and the death and resurrection of Jesus—and how it changes your story?

Have you ever looked back and seen how God has redeemed each moment of your life for your good and His glory?

_____

_____

_____

_____

Fly: We were made for stories. We love the epic battles with enemies and heroes, highs and lows, and characters who overcome their fate and win. Just check out the movie selection on Netflix if you don't believe me.

We were created for stories. We have storylines whether we think so or not. We may call them strongholds, but these are simply stories we believe based on our experiences. But sometimes those storylines are wrong and keep us from the glorious life God has for us. We can change these stories and make them line up with the message of Christ and God's plan. We can allow God to show us how His love and His ultimate story, the gospel, redeem even the hardest parts of our stories.

121

God revealed to me the process of redeeming my story in Ephesians chapter three. So I reread it and asked God to show me His perspective. Now it's your turn. God will faithfully meet you there. Invite God in to redeem your wrong storylines.

Find a quiet spot where you can spend some time with God. Tell Him you want to see His perception. Tell Him you want Him to redeem your story through His love.

> My response is to get down on my knees before the Father, this magnificent Father who parcels out all heaven and earth. I ask him to strengthen you by his Spirit—not a brute strength but a glorious inner strength—that Christ will live in you as you open the door and invite him in. And I ask him that with both feet planted firmly on love, you'll be able to take in with all followers of Jesus the extravagant dimensions of Christ's love. Reach out and experience the breadth! Test its length! Plumb the depths! Rise to the heights! Live full lives, full in the fullness of God.
>
> God can do anything, you know—far more than you could ever imagine or guess or request in your wildest dreams! He does it not by pushing us around but by working within us, his Spirit deeply and gently within us. (Ephesians 3:14–20 MSG)

First reach out to experience "the breadth of His love." Where was He during the painful times that have written lies on your heart? What did He see?

Then test "the length of His love." How far did He go to win you back? Can you now see how far in the future He began working these things out for your good?

Then plumb "the depths of His love." How much did He love you, even in your own dark pit?

Then let's rise to the heights with Him, knowing these things are gone for good because of what He has done. Forgiven. Loved. So very loved.

Your story shows the redeeming power of God's love. This is the fullness of life, the power that comes from God. The good news of the life saved by grace and ready to glorify Him in amazing ways.

After I let God redeem my story, I felt overwhelmingly and unconditionally loved. This made my heart rest in a deeper peace than I had yet experienced. When I learned to start my day by acknowledging His relentlessly pursuant love, the race became easier to run. It was like putting on the right shoes for the marathon of life.

These are the shoes of peace in the armor of God that prepare us for the steps we will take in the journey. When the gospel of peace has made us fully loved and free, we can walk into each new day with a redeemed past and an unlimited future. So print your story and read it each time you start to live in the past. God has redeemed you and calls you forward. He is redeeming new things right now.

Encouragement: "Has the Lord redeemed you? Then speak out! Tell others he has redeemed you from your enemies" (Psalm 107:2 NLT). For encouragement and an example, I have included my redeemed story in an appendix at the back of this book. I pray it will encourage you to see the redemptive power of God's love in the story He is writing for you.

Let's Pray: *Father,* You are the Creator of my story of amazing love. Help me rewrite any wrong parts of my story as I view my experiences through the lens of Your love, shown in Your sacrifice for me when I did not deserve it. I want to be a part of Your story of love by knowing the truth You have revealed in Your Word and Your actions, letting it rewrite my individual story. In Jesus's name, amen.

Write your own prayer here:

Section 4

LEARNING TO BREATHE IN NEW WAYS

*You'll need them throughout your life. God's Word is an
indispensable weapon. In the same way, prayer is essential
in this ongoing warfare. Pray hard and long. Pray for
your brothers and sisters. Keep your eyes open. Keep each
other's spirits up so that no one falls behind or drops out.*
Ephesians 6:17–18 MSG

WHEN I DECIDED TO BELIEVE God about my identity and give Him my whole life, He came through in a powerful way. He revealed my purpose and set me on a new path. Better yet, He gave me the daily armor I need to walk in it.

Several months into the journey, when God moved me into a new work role that was more suited for me, He gave me a vision to help others through my gift of writing. In a moment of radical faith, I signed up for a Christian writing conference I had always wanted to attend.

I'd always had a secret desire to write and help others, but I had been so caught up in the world's measure of success and the Enemy's lies, I had buried that dream. By freeing me to follow Him, God brought purpose and meaning back to my life and restored my dreams. He'd placed my dreams for my life there for His glory and to make me feel alive. He also gave me the tools to keep walking in my aspirations as the battle raged. That is how good God is. When we seek first His kingdom, He gives us the desires of our hearts and equips us to walk in them.

However this did not mean I suddenly conquered my flesh and the attempts of the Enemy to derail me. In fact, quite the opposite happened. The closer I got to walking in my created self, the more Satan increased his assaults. He knew I was becoming a powerful force for the kingdom of light as I increasingly believed God about who I am.

I realized I desperately needed to spend more time with God so I could continue on this new path with Him. I needed to continue to breathe in the breath of life and expel the darkness.

Wielding the shield of faith, helmet of salvation, and sword of the Spirit is a daily battle. We must choose to don the helmet and pick up the shield. Hardest of all, we must choose each day to take up the sword of the Spirit and fight off the world and the lies.

God taught me a few things about choosing to step into the battle every day while He worked ahead of me to bring about His great plan. I had to learn to walk in God's freedom, the abundant life He mentions, as I kept living my normal life.

Being fully known and fully loved is a great first step. But I learned firsthand that the battle rages on after our new identities are built. We must continue to live in the broken world and grapple with the shrewd Enemy for the rest of our time on earth. We move closer to glory as we follow God, but there is no finish line on this side of heaven. There is only the journey and the promise that, although we face trouble in this world, we are never alone. The One who walks with us is the same One who overcame the world.

This final section will be about defining and owning the purpose for which God created us and applying the armor to defend that purpose. The final three pieces of armor—the shield of faith, helmet of salvation, and sword of the Spirit—are the defensive weapons we need for the battle we will face every day for the rest of our lives.

Some days we will crush it, and some days we will not. That's okay. We get to pick up our shield of faith, put on our helmet of salvation, and swing the sword of the Spirit, which is the Word of God, again the next day. So give yourself another big break and learn to live in God's freedom by letting Him show you the way to abundant life.

SOUL ON FIRE

In light of all this, here's what I want you to do.
While I'm locked up here, a prisoner for the Master,
I want you to get out there and walk—better yet, run!—
on the road God called you to travel. I don't want any of
you sitting around on your hands. I don't want anyone
strolling off, down some path that goes nowhere.
And mark that you do this with humility and
discipline—not in fits and starts, but steadily, pouring
yourselves out for each other in acts of love, alert at
noticing differences and quick at mending fences.
Ephesians 4:1–3 MSG

At the writing conference God led me to attend, surrounded by eight hundred other women who also felt called to write or speak for God, I knew I was exactly where I was supposed to be. Instead of feeling competitive or out of place, despite not having had anything published at that point, I felt even more convicted that I was to begin my writing calling. Starting with the story of my demotion experience. I felt more confident of the call on my life than I ever had before, and I had a strong connection to other women I met there who felt the same way. This conference was the best thing I had ever done for God and myself. It was my most faith-filled and obedient act ever, even more so than quitting my job, because believing God called me to something other than a job is something else entirely. And He honored my faithfulness with indescribable joy.

Until now, I tried to tamp down the feeling that I was created for a special purpose. I had known for years that I loved to write, but it seemed ridiculous and arrogant to think God had given me special gifts and called me to do something special with those gifts. But my restless feeling drove my searching. I had tried to make my career my purpose, while God was preparing a new calling for me. And I had been aching to find my purpose.

I finally accepted the calling to write at the conference and I rejoiced with a freedom that had been bottled up for years. Like a shaken soda, it bubbled and fizzed out as I loosened the cap I had tightly shut, due to fear and wrong beliefs. And once it was opened, I found the glorious life that Paul wrote about from prison. This life has nothing to do with current circumstances and everything to do with finding and faithfully believing the purpose etched into my soul.

And then guess what happened when I returned home to all my people, places, and things? Life happened. I came home to an overwhelmingly messy house and a work inbox that scrolled for pages. People needed my attention now. I felt overwhelmed, anxious, and grouchy before I'd been home a week. I became what my family endearingly refers to as "grumpy pants."

The truth is, God gives us all gifts. We are all called to glorify Him and promote His kingdom on earth, even as we stumble through life, making mistakes and living in the monotony of the everyday. Gifts are a part of our unique makeup and the purpose our souls long for, but we are broken and in need of a Savior. It takes a strong faith to stand in this purpose as the broken world rages on. I know from experience that the Enemy will attack even harder as you get closer to your created purpose. He does not like you walking in your purpose for the kingdom of God. It is bad news for his kingdom of darkness.

If you, like me, have been doubting you are specially created and given a unique task, you are hurting your core identity and not walking in the glorious life God has for you. We cannot ignore or run from our created purpose and still feel contented and joyful. Walking in our gifts and fulfilling our unique purpose brings the glorious life God planned for us. This is why, in our culture, we search for identity and purpose. We know we are created for something specific, but we buy into the lie that finding and living our purpose cannot be this easy. It takes a strong defense to protect this calling.

And we know that God causes everything to work together for the good of those who love God and are called according to his purpose for them.
Romans 8:28

Back home, with my family and the work that feeds my family, it sometimes still feels odd to believe I am special to God and that He has a specific plan for me to further His kingdom. But as I get more used to this truth, I can usually push through the monotony of everyday life and the Enemy's lies and believe. I like feeling purposeful. It fills monotonous days with hope. It frees and fulfills me. My heart comes alive when I write and lean into God's Word. And, as Paul states in Ephesians chapter one, I have endless energy and boundless strength, even on hard days.

This must be faith.

Reflect: Due to cultural lies and the lies I believed about myself, I had not thought about my dream of writing in

I am called

years. As a kid, I loved to write and began journaling every day. But I had relegated this gift to the past and never considered letting anyone else see my work. God wanted me to see this gift as a way to illuminate His truth and glorify Him with my life. He wanted me to begin my writing career and had given me the story to do so.

Have you ever had that restless feeling that you were created for more but feel that maybe you've missed it somehow?

_____

_____

_____

_____

_____

_____

Have you given up on some dreams in pursuit of just making it in our world?

_____

_____

_____

_____

_____

_____

The Good Shepherd

Learning Love: Paul the Preacher and Tentmaker

Clearly our hearts are wired for purpose. It seems everyone talks about purpose today, even in our secular culture. We take personality tests and job-aptitude tests, but we keep searching as if our purpose is hidden and as if only a few lucky ones find it. We treat giftings and purpose as mysteries in the church as well. And we think pastors are the only ones with a calling.

These are wrong beliefs. According to the Bible, God has given gifts to all of us. And those gifts help us accomplish our purpose, which is to glorify God and lead others to Him. God willingly and generously gives wisdom and insight to those who ask, not withholding any good thing from us (James 1:5).

We won't fulfill our purpose if we don't believe that God gives us His wisdom and wants the best for us. Our culture equates identity with work. Our spiritual gifts do help us with our work, but we must also use them to glorify God. We need to give up the separation-of-church-and-state mentality and instead live for God in all we do.

The apostle Paul, after his conversion and his call to preach, made tents as his primary means of provision before his imprisonment. And he said the most amazing thing about his job—it provided for his needs and put him in touch with others so he could spread the good news (1 Corinthians 9:15). His primary purpose was to spread the gospel and working diligently to support himself was part of that. It gave him a platform for winning people to Jesus.

> And after Silas and Timothy came down from Macedonia, Paul spent all his time preaching the word. He testified to the Jews that Jesus was the Messiah. But when they opposed and insulted him, Paul shook the dust from his clothes and said, "Your blood is upon your own heads—I am innocent. From now on I will go preach to the Gentiles."
>
> Then he left and went to the home of Titius Justus, a Gentile who worshiped God and lived next door to the synagogue. Crispus, the leader of the synagogue, and everyone in his household believed in the Lord. Many others in Corinth also heard Paul, became believers, and were baptized.
>
> One night the Lord spoke to Paul in a vision and told him, "Don't be afraid! Speak out! Don't be silent! For I am with you, and no one will attack and harm you, for many people in this city belong to me." So Paul stayed there for the next year and a half, teaching the word of God. (Acts 18:5–11 NLT)

After God called Paul, He continued to lead him into new seasons and new places. Paul wasn't called to do only one thing. Rather, he followed God's leading and used the gifts God had given him.

Acts 18:9 tells us, "One night the Lord spoke to Paul in a vision and told him, "Don't be afraid! Speak out! Don't be silent!" During opposition, God encourages Paul in a vision. We, too, are to remain open to God's leading. In Acts 18:21 Paul says, "As he left, however, he said, 'I will come back later, God willing.' Then he set sail from Ephesus." Paul is a great example of doing the will of God rather than the will of others.

Finding Freedom: Finding Your Calling—The Shield of Faith

Release: Do you remember things you wanted to do when you were a child, back when you believed anything was possible? God wrote those dreams on your heart. Name them here:

_____

_____

_____

_____

_____

_____

Fly: Read what Paul says about gifts from Ephesians chapter 4.

> In light of all this, here's what I want you to do. While I'm locked up here, a prisoner for the Master, I want you to get out there and walk—better yet, run!—on the road God called you to travel. I don't want any of you sitting around on your hands. I don't want anyone strolling off, down some path that goes nowhere. And mark that you do this with humility and discipline—not in fits and starts, but steadily, pouring yourselves out for each other in acts of love, alert at noticing differences and quick at mending fences.

You were all called to travel on the same road and in the same direction, so stay together, both outwardly and inwardly. You have one Master, one faith, one baptism, one God and Father of all, who rules over all, works through all, and is present in all. Everything you are and think and do is permeated with Oneness.

But that doesn't mean you should all look and speak and act the same. Out of the generosity of Christ, each of us is given his own gift. The text for this is,

He climbed the high mountain,
He captured the enemy and seized the booty,
He handed it all out in gifts to the people.

Is it not true that the One who climbed up also climbed down, down to the valley of earth? And the One who climbed down is the One who climbed back up, up to highest heaven. He handed out gifts above and below, filled heaven with his gifts, filled earth with his gifts. He handed out gifts of apostle, prophet, evangelist, and pastor-teacher to train Christ's followers in skilled servant work, working within Christ's body, the church, until we're all moving rhythmically and easily with each other, efficient and graceful in response to God's Son, fully mature adults, fully developed within and without, fully alive like Christ.

No prolonged infancies among us, please. We'll not tolerate babes in the woods, small children who are an easy mark for impostors. God wants us to grow up, to know the whole truth and tell it in love—like Christ in everything. We take our lead from Christ, who is the source of everything we do. He keeps us in step with each other. His very breath and blood flow through us, nourishing us so that we will grow up healthy in God, robust in love. (Ephesians 4:1–16 MSG)

We learn from Ephesians 4:7–9 that God gives us the right gifts for the work He has planned for us. Paul also teaches us that it is important for us to know what our gifts are so we can use them to further His kingdom.

Below is a list of spiritual giftings listed in the Bible. Circle the ones that sound like you and then evaluate your results with one of your close friends and family. I found that my spiritual gifts are exhortation, administration, leadership, teaching, word of knowledge, and words of wisdom. And I found that I use these gifts in both my place of work and in the ministry. God has equipped me for both tasks this season.

Administration

The gift of administration is the divine strength or ability to organize multiple tasks and groups of people to accomplish these tasks.

Luke 14:28–30; Acts 6:1–7; 1 Corinthians 12:28

Apostleship

The gift of apostleship is the divine strength or ability to pioneer new churches and ministries through planting, overseeing, and training.

Acts 15:22–35; 1 Corinthians 12:28; 2 Corinthians 12:12; Galatians 2:7–10; Ephesians 4:11–14

Craftsmanship

The gift of craftsmanship is the divine strength or ability to plan, build, and work with your hands in construction environments to accomplish multiple ministry applications.

Exodus 30:22, 31:3–11; 2 Chronicles 34:9–13; Acts 18:2–3

Discernment

The gift of discernment is the divine strength or ability to spiritually identify falsehood, to distinguish between right and wrong motives and the spiritual forces at work in situations.

Matthew 16:21–23; Acts 5:1–11, 16:16–18; 1 Corinthians 12:10; 1 John 4:1–6

Evangelism

The gift of evangelism is the divine strength or ability to help non-Christians take the necessary steps to becoming born-again Christians.

Acts 8:5–6, 8:26–40, 14:21, 21:8; Ephesians 4:11–14

Exhortation

The gift of exhortation is the divine strength or ability to strengthen, comfort or urge others to action through the written or spoken word and biblical truth.

Acts 14:22; Romans 12:8; 1 Timothy 4:13; Hebrews 10:24–25

Faith

The gift of faith is the divine strength or ability to believe in God for unseen supernatural results in every arena of life.

Acts 11:22–24; Romans 4:18–21; 1 Corinthians 12:9; Hebrews 11

Giving

The gift of giving is the divine strength or ability to produce wealth and to give by tithes and offerings for the purpose of advancing the kingdom of God on earth.

Mark 12:41–44; Romans 12:8; 2 Corinthians 8:1–7, 9:2–7 65

Healing

The gift of healing is the divine strength or ability to act as an intermediary in faith and prayer, and by the laying-on of hands for the healing of physical, mental, and spiritual sickness.

Acts 3:1–10, 9:32–35, 28:7–10; 1 Corinthians 12:9, 28

Helps

The gift of helps is the divine strength or ability to work in a supportive role for the accomplishment of tasks in Christian ministry with the ability to often see the need before others do.

Mark 15:40–41; Acts 9:36; Romans 16:1–2; 1 Corinthians 12:28

Hospitality

The gift of hospitality is the divine strength or ability to create warm, welcoming environments for others in places, such as your home, office, or church.

Acts 16:14–15; Romans 12:13, 16:23; Hebrews 13:1–2; 1 Peter 4:9

Intercession

The gift of intercession is the divine strength or ability to stand in the gap in prayer for someone, something, or someplace, believing for profound results.

Hebrews 7:25; Colossians 1:9–12, 4:12–13; James 5:14–16

Word of Knowledge

The gift of knowledge is the divine strength or ability to bring truth to a situation by supernatural revelation. This is often accompanied by a word from God.

Acts 5:1–11; 1 Corinthians 12:8; Colossians 2:2–3

Leadership

The gift of leadership is the divine strength or ability to influence people at their levels while directing and focusing them on the big picture, vision, or idea.

Romans 12:8; 1 Timothy 3:1–13, 5:17; Hebrews 13:17

Mercy

The gift of mercy is the divine strength or ability to feel empathy and to care for those who are hurting in any way.

Matthew 9:35–36; Mark 9:41; Romans 12:8; 1 Thessalonians 5:14

Miracles

The gift of miracles is the divine strength or ability to alter the natural outcomes of life in a supernatural way through prayer, faith, and divine direction.

Acts 9:36–42, 19:11–12, 20:7–12; Romans 15:18–19; 1 Corinthians 12:10, 28

Pastor/Shepherd

The gift of pastor/shepherd is the divine strength or ability to care for the personal needs of others by nurturing and mending life issues.

John 10:1–18; Ephesians 4:11–14; 1 Timothy 3:1–7; 1 Peter 5:1–3

Prophecy

The gift of prophecy is the divine strength or ability to communicate God's truth and heart in a way that calls people to a right relationship with God.

Acts 2:37–40, 7:51–53, 26:24–29; 1 Corinthians 14:1–4; 1 Thessalonians 1:5

Service

The gift of serving is the divine strength or ability to do small or great tasks in working for the overall good of the body of Christ.

Acts 6:1–7; Romans 12:7; Galatians 6:10; 1 Timothy 1:16–18; Titus 3:14

Teaching

The gift of teaching is the divine strength or ability to study and learn from the Scriptures primarily to bring understanding and depth to other Christians.

Acts 18:24–28, 20:20–21; 1 Corinthians 12:28; Ephesians 4:11–14

Tongues (and Interpretation)

The gift of tongues is the divine strength or ability to pray in a heavenly language to encourage your spirit and to commune with God. The gift of tongues is often accompanied by interpretation and should be used appropriately.

Acts 2:1–13; 1 Corinthians 12:10, 14:1–14

Word of Wisdom

The gift of wisdom is the divine strength or ability to understand and to bring clarity to situations and circumstances often through applying the truths of Scripture in a practical way.

Acts 6:3,10; 1 Corinthians 2:6–13, 12:8

God will use your spiritual gifts in different ways throughout your life. You'll grow in your gifting as you spend time with God. Also remember, your calling is not a mystery. Ask God what your spiritual gifts are and how you can use them to glorify Him. Then write them down as a calling statement and believe Him.

YOU ARE LOVED AND FREE

This is my calling statement: I am called to illuminate God's truth in written and spoken words that inspire, encourage, and affirm others to live as the loved and free children of God they were created to be.

Write your spiritual gifts and calling statement below.

My Spiritual Gifts:

_____

_____

My Calling Statement:

_____

_____

_____

_____

I revisit my gifts and my calling statement often because I sometimes doubt they are true. I have written them in the front of my planner. Sometimes I read them daily. When hard times come and I question my worth and purpose again, I remember that God has gifted me and called me to a specific purpose. When the Enemy hurls lies at me, trying to make me stand down, I read through my gifts and calling statement until I hear God's words instead. Believing I am called to a specific purpose is my shield of faith. It is the faith I need to keep walking in the life God planned for me as the battle for my soul rages on.

Encouragement: "The Lord is my strength and shield. I trust him with all my heart. He helps me, and my heart is filled with joy. I burst out in songs of thanksgiving" (Psalm 28:7 NLT).

Let's Pray: *Lord,* thank You for calling each of us to a specific purpose. Your plan is better than anything we could ask or imagine and sets our hearts ablaze. Thank You for the shield of faith. Without the measure of faith You have given, we could never continue in Your way. Continually give us the faith we need to keep following You as the battle rages on. In Jesus's name, amen.

Write your own prayer here:

_____

_____

_____

_____

_____

_____

_____

_____

_____

_____

_____

_____

KEEPING COMPANY WITH HIM

Keep company with him and learn a life of love. Observe
how Christ loved us. His love was not cautious but extrav-
agant. He didn't love in order to get something from us
but to give everything of himself to us. Love like that.
Ephesians 5:2 MSG

TRYING TO WALK IN FAITH and keep the momentum going, I pushed
through the weeks after the conference. I wanted to finish the
book and get it magically published so I could go on a road tour,
preaching the message to thousands of people that they are loved
and free in Christ. I also wanted to immediately be an expert at my
new job, crushing new initiatives and making great things happen.

I am a fairly idealistic person, and I form lofty goals when I get
passionate about something, especially something new. I wanted to
show God and everyone that I believed in His calling and the new
path He had for me and that I was strong enough to get it all done.
I tried to push through the hardship of starting the new season
and the uncertainty of how it would all work out. I tried to push

through dozens of doubts and the exhaustion from pretending all was well, even though it wasn't.

But I was gripped by fear again, meditating on false thoughts and feelings. My new role was rather ambiguous, and I felt as if I was flailing in the wind. Overachievers despise that feeling more than anything. And I was trying to hang onto my belief that God had called me to write for Him. But He was silent. I didn't know what to do. Fear and negativity poured into my thoughts, feelings, and actions. They were a yellow, flashing caution light, telling me to slow down.

I had slipped right back into my old habits of making these new tasks (finishing the book and trying to excel at my new job) speak to my worth. Satan used these new, good things to try to take me out again.

This is one of the problems of being a born achiever living in a society that applauds achievements. Even when they are God's assignments, the accomplishment doesn't add value to my worth, and it doesn't change God's love for me. But it's hard to recognize the Enemy's sly tactics because his lies almost sound like truth. And what better way to introduce doubts than to convince me to run back to my old habits, believing I had gotten it all wrong?

However God has shown me that this is spiritual warfare that I will fight all my life and that I cannot win these battles alone. When I try to fight my achievement-centric tendencies in my own strength, it results in negative thoughts, feelings, and actions. I get defeated, then doubtful and bitter rather quickly.

Winning daily battles changes my heart and ways. It's not a one-time, magical prayer. Lies and lifestyles are burned into me from the culture around me and from lies I have believed during hard times. And the Enemy knows this and is skilled in using these lies against me. I know from experience that I am not aware of all the broken places in my heart, but Satan sure is.

I am still quite a mess at times. But when I finally fall to my knees again, refusing to try to push through my challenges alone, I can rest with God. He loves me as I am and wants to fight with me for the rest of my life, helping me sort out my mess until the day He calls me home.

When I choose to keep company with Him despite my pages-long to-do list, He shows me His easier way. I find freedom in the already-won battle. I find strength that fuels me to begin again. I find grace to right all my wrong actions and to overcome

Each time he said. "My grace is all you need. My power works best in weakness." So now I am glad to boast about my weaknesses, so that the power of Christ can work through me.
2 Cor 12:9

shame. Best of all, I find a love so extravagant it fills me up again so I can pour it out for Him.

I find all these things simply by choosing to keep company with Him.

Reflect: When hardships set in, I almost fell into the devil's trap of believing I misheard God and was not loved and free in Christ. I wanted the new season

In Him, I am strong

to be easier, as if that would help me believe it was true. But that's not how it works. God has called us to faithfulness in the daily battle and to rest in him as our armor and source of strength.

When hardships set in, do you doubt God has called you?

_____

_____

_____

_____

During difficult times, do you slip back into old habits and believe old lies?

_____

_____

_____

_____

_____

_____

Learning Love: Choosing the Best Thing

We certainly live in a busy era and the Enemy has always used busyness to keep us distracted and far from God. He knows we can find unstoppable power if we keep regular company with Jesus, which we can learn from the story of Mary and Martha.

> As Jesus and the disciples continued on their way to Jerusalem, they came to a certain village where a woman named Martha welcomed him into her home. Her sister, Mary, sat at the Lord's feet, listening to what he taught. But Martha was distracted by the big dinner she was preparing. She came to Jesus and said, "Lord,

doesn't it seem unfair to you that my sister just sits here while I do all the work? Tell her to come and help me."

But the Lord said to her, "My dear Martha, you are worried and upset over all these details! There is only one thing worth being concerned about. Mary has discovered it, and it will not be taken away from her." (Luke 10:38–42)

Martha is like me and strives to please Jesus by doing things for Him. In this case, she is working hard to cook an extravagant meal for Him. She gets bitter that Mary is not helping her and confronts Jesus about it. He responds with something we all need to remember when we work so hard that we get bitter: "'Martha, dear Martha, you're fussing far too much and getting yourself worked up over nothing. One thing only is essential, and Mary has chosen it—it's the main course, and won't be taken from her'" (Luke 10:42 MSG).

This is simple, profound, and hard. Notice that Jesus is gracious to Martha. He knows this is a human condition, and He is not angry or disappointed with her. He calls her "dear" because, although she'd missed the mark, He loves her, and He wants her free to be with Him.

We all know we are not worthy to come to God, so we work to try to become worthy. God says, "No, I sent my Son to cover you and make you worthy as you are. Just come and sit at My feet, learn from Me, and fill yourself with My love. This is the only essential thing. The best thing."

Finding Freedom: Make Time to be with God—The Helmet of Salvation

Release: What feelings or actions indicate that you might be in battle by yourself?

_____

_____

_____

_____

What are some ways you can combat busyness and start spending more time with God?

_____

_____

_____

_____

Fly: Read what Paul says about spending time with the Lord.

> Watch what God does, and then you do it, like children who learn proper behavior from their parents. Mostly what God does is love you. Keep company

with him and learn a life of love. Observe how Christ loved us. His love was not cautious but extravagant. He didn't love in order to get something from us but to give everything of himself to us. Love like that.

Don't drink too much wine. That cheapens your life. Drink the Spirit of God, huge draughts of him. Sing hymns instead of drinking songs! Sing songs from your heart to Christ. Sing praises over everything, any excuse for a song to God the Father in the name of our Master, Jesus Christ. (Ephesians 5:1–2, 18–20 MSG)

It's easy for the Enemy to keep us focused on busyness instead of God. When your eyes are off God, Satan has a better chance of making you forget how much He loves you and has freed you. Then the Enemy can speak lies, which become bad actions.

But when we spend time with God, He renews our mind, and we forget the lies. This is your helmet of salvation. Remember, you were saved to live in a close relationship with God. Keep company with Him, and He will restore you.

The key is choosing to spend time with God—not doing, but just being. I spend my lunch hour with Him. It is a sacrifice for me to break away from my achievement mindset in the middle of my work day. I do this by reading a devotional and journaling my prayers. This is one of the most restful and rewarding hours of my day. It's sometimes hard to take a break and spend time with God, but He is pleased with this sacrifice, and it ends up being an amazing time of refreshment.

You can also spend time with the Lord by reading His Word, either through a Bible reading plan or Bible study. You could take a prayer walk outside if the weather is nice, or find a private place to pray. Praying is simply talking to God, knowing He listens and cares about your concerns, and believing He will respond in His way at the right time. There is no right or wrong way to pray. The best prayers come from an honest heart. I recommend reading the Bible and praying every day.

When is the best time for you to spend with God? Think about your typical day. When are you busiest, pushing through to finish your to-do list? This is probably a great time to add purposeful time with God. You might fear you won't get through your to-do list if you take time out to have a quiet time with Him. I used to feel the same way, but God showed me it's not true. I give Him time, and somehow He gives it back threefold.

Try it. You will not be disappointed.

Encouragement: "Ask and it will be given to you; seek and you will find; knock and the door will be opened to you. For everyone who asks receives; the one who seeks finds; and to the one who knocks, the door will be opened" (Matthew 7:7–8 NIV).

Let's Pray: *God*, You are faithful to meet us any time we come to You in prayer. Help us to learn to spend time with You. This is what our souls were designed for and need most of all. Thank You for Your grace and all-sufficiency for everything we could ever need. In Jesus's name, amen.

Write your own prayer here:

_____

_____

_____

_____

_____

_____

FULL CIRCLE

And that about wraps it up. God is strong, and he wants
you strong. So take everything the Master has set out for
you, well-made weapons of the best materials. And put
them to use so you will be able to stand up to everything
the Devil throws your way. This is no afternoon athletic
contest that we'll walk away from and forget about in a
couple of hours. This is for keeps, a life-or-death fight to
the finish against the Devil and all his angels.
Ephesians 6:10–12 MSG

AND THE BATTLE RAGES ON . . .

In this broken world, things break every day. My car broke down today, just after I made the investment to get this book to print. And I am not going to lie and say my faith can fully overcome the fear this brings. It can't. I'm not there yet. I don't expect to be, but I'm doing better than I used to because I now know none of this defines me and none of this has the power to overcome the good life God has planned for me.

Just two weeks ago, as I struggled to decide if investing in this book was God's will, fear and doubts raged in my head. But God led me back to the place where He first asked me to share this message: a great tree on a mountain-bike trail in my southwest Colorado town. This tree is more than the tallest twisted pinyon pine I have ever seen. It's where I buried all the lies on Good Friday, 2019. It's where I realized my worth isn't based on others' opinions of me or on my accomplishments.

I needed this reminder again as I began to feel fear about the book, the new job, and the car. I want so badly to take control of this fear, figure out the future, and follow the right steps so people will buy the book and I can succeed in my new job. But the success of this book and my performance in my new job do not define me. Neither does the car I drive, which is good because all I can afford right now is a beater.

No matter how hard I hustle through this life, I can't add significance to myself. I can't because I am already as significant as I can be. I was created on purpose and with a purpose by the God of the universe, and He loves me. Not because of what I do or don't do. Not because of how my life turned out this week, this year, or this decade. I am as loved today as I will ever be because I am a dearly loved child of God. I was born loved, and nothing I do adds to His love for me.

His unconditional love sets me free. As I let it wash over me again, I know I am saved and set free, not so I can do more works, but so I can have a relationship with God and learn from Him, becoming what He already sees in me. It's His doing. I am filled with the Holy Spirit by faith alone. It is a gift to me, and it's everything I need.

So I cut down the lies. I don't need to accomplish anything to make myself more loved. I could not possibly be more loved than I already am.

I am loved and free. God's Word tells me so, and His Spirit

confirms it again as I sit under this tree, reread the truth in His Word, and let it into my heart.

For the word of God is alive and powerful. It is sharper than the sharpest two-edged sword, cutting between soul and spirit, between joint and marrow. It exposes our innermost thoughts and desires.
Heb 4:12

The Bible is my sword, my greatest weapon for the war raging for my soul every day. It says I am a dearly loved child of God (1 John 3:1), fearfully and wonderfully made (Psalm 139:14), redeemed by His blood (Ephesians 1:7), and called to follow Him forevermore (Romans 8:28). So I cut down all the lies and pretenses that do not line up with Bible truths. The truth is simply that I am loved and free.

Reflect: How are you doing with this message that you are loved and free?

I am Loved & Free

_____

_____

_____

_____

Which truth do you struggle with the most today?

_____

_____

_____

_____

_____

Learning Love: The Word of God

All Scripture is God-breathed and is useful for teaching,
rebuking, correcting and training in righteousness, so that
the servant of God may be thoroughly equipped
for every good work.
2 Timothy 3:16–17 NIV

The Bible is a long book with stories about real people, with many authors and several styles. But it has one central message. God made the world, and He created humans in His image to live in relationship with Him. He loves us so much that when we exercised our free will and sinned against Him, He came to rescue us and restore us to our original created state through the death of His Son on the cross.

Finding Freedom: Live in the Word—the Sword of the Spirit

Release: Do you have the habit of reading God's Word every day?

_____

_____

_____

What are some ways you can start applying the Word of God to your life?

_____

_____

_____

_____

_____

_____

Fly: Read here what Paul says about the whole armor of God.

> A final word: Be strong in the Lord and in his mighty power. Put on all of God's armor so that you will be able to stand firm against all strategies of the devil. For we are not fighting against flesh-and-blood enemies, but against evil rulers and authorities of the unseen world, against mighty powers in this dark world, and against evil spirits in the heavenly places.
>
> Therefore, put on every piece of God's armor so you will be able to resist the enemy in the time of evil. Then after the battle you will still be standing firm. Stand your ground, putting on the belt of truth and the body armor of God's righteousness. For shoes, put on the peace that comes from the Good News so that you will be fully prepared. In addition to all of these, hold up the shield of faith to stop the fiery arrows of the devil. Put on salvation as your helmet, and take the sword of the Spirit, which is the word of God.
>
> Pray in the Spirit at all times and on every occasion. Stay alert and be persistent in your prayers for all believers everywhere. (Ephesians 6:10–18)

The Enemy attacks each day, and he is cunning. He is the deceiver and he knows how to twist the truth just enough to make you believe it. Our greatest weapon against his lies is the truth that God provides us in His Word. It says His Word is sharper than any two-edged sword and has the power to cut through lies (Hebrews 4:12).

How do we wield this weapon against Satan? We meditate on the truth by getting into the Word every day and finding the truth that cancels the lies.

I started this journey nine months ago. Every day, I have to put on the armor God helped me build. Sometimes I do this multiple times in a day. That is okay. God is pleased and stays with me in the battle.

Place all the pieces of armor in a place where you can find them easily and use them.

If you question your worth again, read Ephesians chapter one and your manifesto.

If you revert to chasing the world's definition of success, read Ephesians chapter two, surrender to God, and seek His thoughts on the season you're in.

If you feel defeated, read Ephesians chapter three and remember how all the pieces of your life fit into His epic story of love.

If you wonder whether your life matters, read Ephesians chapter four and pick up your shield of faith by reading your calling statement and reminding yourself of the gifts God has given you.

If your thoughts, feelings, and actions don't align with God's truths, read Ephesians chapter five again and remind yourself to rest in Him.

Make it a priority to get into His Word every day. Each book of the Bible has applicable truths. Knowing and believing the Word of God is the weapon you need to fight and win the battle for your identity.

And every day, pray unceasingly (Ephesians 6:18).

Encouragement: If you do not know what to pray, you can always start with the Lord's Prayer (Matthew 6:9–13 NLT).

> **The Lord's Prayer:**
> Our Father in heaven,
> may your name be kept holy.
> May your Kingdom come soon.
> May your will be done on earth,
> as it is in heaven.
> Give us today the food we need,
> and forgive us our sins,
> as we have forgiven those who sin against us.
> And don't let us yield to temptation,
> but rescue us from the evil one. (Matthew 6:9–13 NLT)

Let's Pray: *Lord,* help us to live in Your Word every day. We find the truth of who we are and who You are in Your Word. Help us apply these truths to our lives so we can live in the truth that sets us free. Thank You for Your Word and the Spirit, who helps us understand it. In Jesus's name, amen.

Write your own prayer here:

_____

_____

_____

_____

_____

_____

FINAL WORDS

THE WON BATTLE

WELCOME TO THE WON BATTLE. I pray this time of sowing will continue to produce amazing fruit in your life. The battle will rage on, but you have everything you need in God to keep winning. Even on days when *you* don't win the battle for your identity, God does. He already created you beautifully and purposefully. Nothing can change that. He already redeemed you fully. It is finished. You are loved and free. The battle is won.

APPENDIX 1

TATTOO THE NAMES OF GOD ON YOUR HEART

El Roi: The God Who Sees Me (Genesis 16:7–13)
Jehovah Shamma: God Is Already There (Jeremiah 23:16–24)
Jehovah Rapha: The Lord My Healer (Exodus 15:22–27)
Jehovah Raah: The Lord My Shepherd (Psalm 23)
El Shaddai: All Sufficient One (Genesis 17: 1–8)
The Way, the Truth, and the Life (John 14:1–14)
Abba: Father (Romans 8:15–17)
Jehovah Jireh: My Provider (1 Timothy 6:13–21)
El Sali: God of My Strength (Psalm 18:1–6)
The Good Shepherd (John 10:11–18)
Jehovah Shalom: God Is My Peace (Romans 16:20–27)
The Word (John 1:1)

APPENDIX 2

MICAH'S REDEEMED STORY: RELENTLESSLY PURSUANT LOVE

The Breadth of My Love

YOU ARE ELEVEN YEARS OLD and I see you, my precious child. I see the tender yet fierce-hearted little girl who just wants the other kids to like her or, at this point, to just leave her alone. Don't believe the other children when they call you names. They are lost and broken too. You don't know what they are going through, but I do. One's parents just got divorced after years of screaming matches. One's older sister torments her. They are all stuck in the world's way of comparing and measuring up, and it is killing them as well. Don't let them tell you who you are. That is my job. I created you. I made you and you are my work of art. You are lovely. I love that you search for great love. I made you that way. My love is what you're searching for. You won't find it in the approval of the other kids. Please don't turn your back. I will be beside you wherever you go, even if you turn your back to me. Someday you will see that. You will look back and see Me always with you.

The Length of My Love

I see you at twenty-one because I am still here, just as I said I would be. I tried to warn you not to marry him. You know this. I know you heard me, but you were scared not to get married. You believed all those things they said about you. It's okay. I work far into the future to make good of all the bad things. I wish you would come home now, but I know you're not ready yet. I'm still working now and in the future to care for you and your daughter. She is my precious child too. I love you more than you disdain me. You're not alone. I know you're scared, but I am here. Even when you think you're alone, I am here. Even when you believe you're unworthy of better, I am here. No matter what you have done, I love you and always will.

The Depth of My Love

Yes I am still here after twenty-four years, and I see you in the depths of the darkness you dug yourself into. I forgive you. I sent my Son to cover all this for you. Don't you see? I knew this would happen. I knew my precious girl would believe the Enemy's lies, turn to false gods of the world, and fall into this pit of death and destruction. You feel completely unworthy, ashamed of all you've done. You are not a lost cause, but you think you're too far gone, that you've messed up everything. You think you're beyond repair. In the pit with nowhere else to turn, you reach for Me, and I am here. You can't see Me through your shame. It's like a black cloud covering your eyes, but I see you reaching, and I'm working it out. As you open the door wider to Me, you'll see that I've been working out a way back to Me—the home your heart desires. Will you follow Me, even as you believe you're not worthy? Even now, covered in the mire of your own sin, I love you and would do anything to get you back home with Me. Reach out and take my hand and let

Me lead you out, for I am with you in the pit. My love is with you in the pit.

The Heights of My Love

I am rejoicing and all of heaven rejoices with Me! You have come home and finally accepted Me back into your heart, and all the angels sing! You feel it in your soul as all of heaven rejoices and redemptive love washes over you. I see you, twenty-five years old now, and I smile at my precious daughter as my love radiates through your heart. You feel my love again because you let me in. You turned around at that church service your friend asked you to, and you opened your eyes to see that I never left you. I never will. I have always loved you, and I always will. As you raised your hand in response to the pastor's invitation, I came to save you and lead you back to your rightful place. Believe that you are saved this moment, no matter what you have done. I have the love you have always searched for. A love so strong it chases you down, never gives up, and always believes in you. A love so powerful it relentlessly pursues you and always will. A love that lives in you as you live in Me. That is your story. Loved. So very loved.

NOTES

[1] Allgifts.com. 2020. https://giftstest.com/allgifts.

ORDER INFORMATION

REDEMPTION PRESS

To order additional copies of this book, please visit
www.redemption-press.com.
Also available on Amazon.com and BarnesandNoble.com
or by calling toll-free 1-844-2REDEEM.

CPSIA information can be obtained
at www.ICGtesting.com
Printed in the USA
LVHW041242280820
664156LV00005B/805